Being Fathered *for a* Divine Purpose

Knowing God as "Papa"

J. Nicole Williamson

Copyright © 2009 by J. Nicole Williamson

Being Fathered for a Divine Purpose
by J. Nicole Williamson

Printed in the United States of America

ISBN 978-1-60791-228-6

All rights reserved solely by the author. The author guarantees all contents are original and do not infringe upon the legal rights of any other person or work. No part of this book may be reproduced in any form, except for brief quotations, without written permission from the author. The views expressed in this book are not necessarily those of the publisher.

Unless otherwise indicated, Scripture quotations are taken from the New American Standard Bible®, Copyright © 1960, 1962, 1963, 1968, 1971, 1972, 1973, 1975, 1977, 1995 by The Lockman Foundation. Used with permission. (www.Lockman.org)

www.xulonpress.com

CONTENTS

Introduction	xi
Father Foundations	13
When Earthly Families Fail	27
Healing Family Wounds	43
You Can Call Him "*PAPA*"	59
Who *is* Your Daddy?	69
The Father and His Sons	79
Dad is There for You	97
Dad's Discipline	117
Our Father's Work	127
The Father's Blessing	141
For Love of the Father	157

Dedication

I dedicate this book to my parents and spiritual leaders whom God has placed in my life throughout the years. Their influence has played an important role in making me who I am today as a daughter of God. I am grateful for their lives.

To my father and mother, Floyd and Venita Bennett, to whom I am most grateful. Thank you, Mom, for everything you and Dad (now with Father God) have been to me. Without you I wouldn't be here! I am thankful for a godly heritage. I cherish every memory of my father and I could have no greater hero and model of faith than you, Mom. I especially hold dear a word Dad once gave me in a dark season of my life: *all things work together for good to those who love God and who are called according to His purpose* (Romans 8:28).

To Dr. R. Edward and Eleanor Miller who are also with the Father today—I am grateful for their lives that were the voice of God's love and inspiration of hope and vision for a life of intimacy with God. I am thankful for the privilege of having known them as spiritual parents who trained, taught, and modeled a life of revival and the presence of God to many around the world.

To Rev. John C. Miller and his wife, Maria—there are no words that can ever convey my gratitude to you both. You were the hands of God who ministered the Light that broke my chains of darkness. You were true spiritual parents who took me in and loved me when

I was lost. Thank you for praying me into the vast realm of divine freedom in Christ. I am eternally indebted.

To Dr. Randy Speed and his wife, Carol, who have trained, nurtured, and led countless people into their divine destiny. You are true shepherds in this generation and highly polished arrows in the Father's quiver that have been sent for such a time as this. Your *fathering* hearts are an inspiration and godly model to the body of Christ, and I am truly grateful for your leadership, wisdom, and ceaseless encouragement.

To my wonderful husband, Ken, who is also the father of our two wonderful children, Daniel and Bethany. Thank you, honey, for your unceasing love and care. Thank you for being a safe place for our family, and for the godly example you have modeled to our son and daughter. I love you.

Foreword

Our Heavenly Father has been raising sons and daughters for thousands of years! He is fully acquainted with our needs and struggles. He is able to bring us from spiritual infancy, through our spiritually formative years, and on to adult *"sonship"*. He knows when our earthly days are finished and it is time to be taken home to glory. Our Father is great! He makes no mistakes. We can be thankful for His purpose for us to be born into the life of a particular nation, race and culture, as well as for the unique set of parents He has given us. He has a sovereign plan for our long-term well-being. We should thank God for our parents and honor them.

The Bible reveals God as the Lord of the universe and calls Him "Father" in both the Old and New Testament. He is the Father and Lord of creation. James describes Him as the "Father of lights". He created the stars as well as the angels. The Old Testament names angels as "the sons of God" (benai elohim). Paul says that every family under heaven is named or set aside for Him (Eph. 3:15).

We all need a caring human father (or an equivalent) as early as possible in our lives to help us understand what God the Father is like as a Person. Remote, indifferent, unavailable human fathers can lead us to believe that God also is detached, unconcerned, and uninvolved in the daily cares of our world. However, the psalmist praises God as a loving Father saying, "Father of the fatherless and protector of widows is God in His holy habitation" (Ps. 10:14). Hosea writes that the fatherless find mercy in Him (Hos. 14:3). God is described in Psalm 10:14 as the one who helps the fatherless. And King David says, "When my father and my mother forsake me, then the LORD will take me up" (Ps. 27:10).

"*Being Fathered for a Divine Purpose*" is a wonderful and insightful book that leads us to the Father's heart. Nicole Williamson has put into words, a true likeness of our God as a caring, loving, and protective "*Papa*". Nicole has written from the Word, from her heart, and from the many experiences of her life. I have known, worked, and ministered with her for close to ten years as a sister in Christ, and an Elder within *The River*. I have watched the calling of God continue to develop her as a gifted teacher, writer, and minister. In this book, Nicole has presented to us as pastors and teachers, to those who enjoy studying, as well as to the reader who just enjoys a good book, a wonderful insight to the Father heart of God.

I invite you to enjoy the journey to living in the heart of our Father. Thank you, Nicole, for this understanding of our Father's heart in *Being Fathered for a Divine Purpose*.

Dr. Randy Speed
Senior Pastor, *River of Glory*
Plano, Texas

Introduction

"But now, O LORD, You are our Father, we are the clay,
And You our potter; and all of us are the work of Your hand."
Isaiah 64:8

I have been a Christian most of my life. I have been involved in music ministry for now over thirty years, have been in places of revival (including Argentina), and am one who is deeply grateful for Jesus' delivering salvation. I hold a Bachelor Degree in Theology, teach, write and love God with all my heart. And yet, amidst all the revelation of God I have received on my journey with Him, I walked many years before I *experienced* the intimate revelation of God as my *Abba Father*. I knew the theology of that truth; I knew He was my Father, but I had never experienced the fellowship of His presence as a loving *"Papa"* until one glorious encounter in December, 1999. Until that day, He had been to me a loving Creator, wonderful God, Master, Potter, Savior, and good Shepherd. However, I had not thought of Him in the light of being my *"Dad."* Yet this was the very message that Jesus brought to mankind and is the heartbeat of Christianity. The way of salvation is meant to bring us into fellowship with God as our *Abba (Papa) Father*.

Sometimes in our Christian life we can overlook the most basic truths and realities that are meant to be the foundation of our walk with God. The revelation of Father God is one of those. The Father didn't send Jesus so that we can have great theology and religion, but a life immersed in the divine reality of relationship with Him as His children—sons and daughters who are fathered for a divine purpose.

While religion reveres God as Supreme, it too often holds Him at a distance, too holy to touch, and too revered to be called *"Dad"*. But it was Jesus who initiated the loving and respectful address of God as *Abba Father;* *"Papa"* or *"Daddy"* is the English equivalent for *"Abba"*. Without question, God *is* holy and we must guard our relationship with Him free from any taint of irreverence. But God also wants us to know that, while holy, He is *Abba Father* to those who are born of His Spirit. The *Almighty One* has invited us into the privilege of knowing Him as *Papa*. He wants our hand to be held by His as we journey through life with Him as His beloved children— offspring who bear His image and minister His kingdom on earth.

In Malachi 4:5, the prophet declared that in the last days there would be a return of the hearts of fathers to their children, and the children to their fathers. Many have termed this current generation in America a "fatherless" one. Many have experienced separation or division in relationship with fathers. Many have been separated from Father God. Since a *return* in relationship can only happen after two have been apart, we are thus poised for a revival and restoration of fathering in this generation. Such a healing begins with a return to the intimate knowledge of God as our *Abba Father*. He will teach us to how to father our homes, cities, and nation.

The world has many leaders, but not many fathers. We are in the last days, and it is time for the revelation of God as our *Abba Father* that man's fatherlessness be healed. The earth itself is groaning with longing for the manifestation of the sons and daughters of God— those who are *"fathered"* by *Abba,* and who, in turn, *"father"* the nations with the healing power of His love. When fathers and children alike experience the Fatherhood of God, they will return to love and honor toward one another. Then, says Malachi, the curse will be removed and the land healed.

The earth needs the healing that can only come by the revelation and return to God as our Father. *"Father, hallowed be Your name. Your kingdom come, Your will be done, on earth as it is in heaven."*

CHAPTER 1

Father Foundations

Two things that most shape our life, choices, and direction are how we are fathered, and how we respond to fathers. This includes parents, spiritual leaders, authority figures, and most of all, God Himself who is the Father of all. Our responses to fathers differ: we love fathers, reject fathers, need fathers, run away from fathers, are hurt by fathers, are encouraged by fathers, are neglected by fathers, and are trained by fathers. But no matter how we have related to them, the bottom line is, if it weren't for our fathers, we wouldn't be here. Fathers are the most significant part of our past, present, and future. And the most significant father of all is Father God.

No matter how old we are, our lives are impacted by fathers—whether it be a dad, a coach, or a spiritual leader. Our relationship with fathers and responses to their leadership (*or* absence of it), influences our own leadership skills with ourselves, our children, within our work environment, ministry, or mentoring relationships. The more we understand our own need for fathering, and how to rightly relate to fathers—and especially to Father God—the more wholeness, fruitfulness, and divine purpose we will know and experience.

Fathers play a central part in our learning to govern in life. God designed a father's presence to be a loving authority and righteous government in our life to train us as a lineage of those who also rightly govern. God created both men *and* women to govern in all aspects of life with divine purpose for a divine destiny (Gen. 1:27-28). Being "fathered" helps both sons and daughters to be better parents, leaders, and influencers—those who shape the destiny of families and communities, and thus nations.

Understanding God's role of fathering us, and how to relate to fathers He has placed in our life, creates a solid foundation for our life and destiny. Over the years, God has helped me to see His fathering care in my life, as well as heal any wrong foundations laid through the way earthly fathers have related to me, and I to them. We will look more at healing family dynamics in the next chapter. But first, let's look at the importance of God's original design regarding fathers and families.

Fathers are Authors and Guardians

The simple definition of a father is that he is an *"author"*: someone who causes something to exist. He is an initiator of life. All the dynamics needed to create life can be set in place, but it is the *father* who ignites the spark that sets life in motion. In Greek, the term *"father"* (*"pater"*) not only refers to the head of a family, but to the *founder* of a society that is **animated by the same spirit as himself**, and for whom he cares in a paternal way with instruction and provision. The term *"father"* is also given to those who cause an idea, discovery, or invention to take on "a life of its own".

A father gives, preserves, and protects life. He is both the *source of identity* for what he brings into existence, as well as being the *gardener and guardian of life*. This was the commission that God gave the first earthly father, Adam. He was to cultivate the earth and begin the multiplication of mankind (Gen. 2:15). He was to rule the earth with the government of God and train up the next generation to do the same. Created in the likeness of God, Adam was to represent God's fathering care and government in the earth. His wife,

Eve, was taken from his side to be his helper in governing the earth regarding the purposes of God (Gen. 2:21-24).

Adam's role as a man was *key* to the life and welfare of succeeding generations. So, too, all fathers hold a dynamic key not only to the existence of the next generation, but to the maturing of their child's success in life, labor, relationships, and divine purpose. Dads, you are important!

A father's involvement impacts the life of his children in areas such as:

- Identity and Security
- Accountability and Ethics
- Guidance and Moral Instruction
- Discipline and Character
- Relationships and Values
- Vocation and Education
- Communication
- Sexuality—both masculinity and femininity

You can see what an essential responsibility fathers have. Father God does not leave fathers to try to do this on their own, but He, as a Father, is man's role model. Men have the Father's Word to teach them and His Spirit to guide them. The Heavenly Father does not leave them to "figure out" such an important work! God's presence and involvement with His sons teaches them how to rightly father *their* children.

Because of a father's position of responsibility in leadership, those under their care are commanded to respect, honor, and support them through loving obedience and prayer (Eph. 6:1; 1 Tim. 2:1-2). I realize in writing this, there are some who have experienced a father's harmful demands that are contrary to God's Word. While such actions *cannot* be supported, we *can* pray for that father. Scripture exhorts those under authority (which includes all mankind) to be honorable with attitudes and actions toward them, and especially toward parents. This is right in the Father's eyes.

While a father's influence creates a foundation for his children of how they should live, even the most perfect parent can't prevent a child's freewill from making wrong choices. Children also have responsibility. Look at Adam and Eve. They had the most perfect *Dad*—God. They had a perfect environment, and were perfectly loved. I'm sure there was not a thing they lacked. And yet, they chose to do the opposite of what God said.

Yes, Father God had trouble with His children, too! And look at the consequence—refusing His instruction led to their suffering ... and the suffering of everything under their care, that being, the whole earth. **Our response to a father's leadership not only impacts our own well-being and destiny, but the well-being of those we *influence.***

Fathering a Child's Destiny

A father's good instruction creates a solid foundation for their children's identity so that they can be released fully into their divine destiny. Children want to know their identity as to who they are not only as family members, but as individuals within the family. Father God intends for a child's special design (God-given identity) to be cultivated through parental training and then *released* with blessing. This Biblical family value was once a foundation of American society. However, this foundation has been consistently attacked through a cultural mindset that has embraced a *spirit of independence*. This mindset seeks "individuality" apart from being *fathered* for their destiny. As our culture has turned away from Father God's instructions and training, it is also evidenced in a general turning away from fathers.

Biblical values establish a mindset of *dependence* on God as the building block for life and family. Biblical values promote unity through honor of authority and personal responsibility; a perspective of individuality, yet as loving *inter*-dependence, not *independence*, and not co-dependence. As Americans, we love independence. Our country was founded on it. We celebrate it every year. We delight to be independent. But if we lift the cover and look inside, we see the *spirit* of independence as one that wars against authority in order to establish *self-rule*.

While we term America's existence as a celebration of independence, the truth is she was born out of a struggle against tyranny—she was fighting for her God-given identity and destiny. She should have been blessed and released, but she wasn't, and so she fought to become who God called her to be. However, Satan, who seeks to devour and destroy divine destiny, saw the open door of celebrated "independence" to establish a *spirit of independence*. God birthed America, but as a child with an independent heart, she has been pushing away God's fathering presence to establish her own identity—an identity that is self-made for self-centered pursuits. Adam and Eve forsook God's instruction and they lost their life. Forsaking righteous instruction always causes a loss of life, and thus a loss of fulfilled destiny.

What about the need for children to grow and become *independent*? Children *do* need to grow into the place of being established into who they are and their *God-given identity*. But a child's true identity is formed and matured by embracing responsibility and parental guidance, not by casting off restraint. And in the proper moment, a child's leaving shouldn't have to be a declaration of independence from their parents, but of being "blessed and sent." **The heart of true fathering calls forth the identity of a child and sends the child into their divine purpose.**

As a youth, I viewed independence and self-rule as the way to find my identity. I grew up in the 1960s and was greatly influenced by a culture in rebellion. But through many hard lessons (and God's mercy!), I learned that perspective was wrong. That path led to a *loss* of identity. It was a path to an identity designed by the god of this world—one whose goal is our destruction. **True identity—one that is divinely unique and laced with purpose—is found through embracing God-given responsibility, especially within family relationships.** Embracing responsibility begins with honoring the righteous instruction of a father. This path trains us for a full and fruitful destiny.

A father's role encourages the full development of a son and daughter so that they are sent out with blessing to *be* a blessing. Psalm

127:3-5 says that children are to be like arrows shot from a father's bow—arrows that hit a specific target. This biblical teaching is the opposite of cultural mindsets that promote "doing our own thing" and leaving to "find our own way". **Father God has established that children should be *trained* and *sent* with divine purpose into divine destiny.** This is how He fathers us!

Old Testament Model of Fathers

In the Old Testament, the Mid-Eastern philosophy of the family was that of being a small kingdom within itself with the father being the *supreme ruler, priest of the family, military leader, judge, and disciplinarian.*[1]

- As *supreme ruler,* the father's authority covered everyone in the household, including the wife, children, grandchildren, servants, etc. Every tribe, community, family, or even company of travelers had a "father" who was the head of the group. Under the father's leadership, the mother was also a representative of God in the matter of authority. She, too, carried a title of honor.
- As the *priest of the family,* the father established the family as a corporate place of worship.
- As the *military leader, judge, and disciplinarian,* the father formed the family as a civil community. As such, children learned discipline, justice, and warfare against raiding tribes.

(Note: Children need to learn not only discipline, but warfare. Life is full of battles! We wage war on many fronts for success in life. Scripture says that our struggle is not against flesh and blood, but against spiritual rulers, powers, world forces of darkness, and spiritual forces of wickedness in heavenly places—Eph. 6:12. A child's first training in spiritual warfare should be through mom and dad.)

While the father was the highest authority of the family, *the entire family functioned together as a united community.* This helped to give personal security, maintain family traditions, and release sons and daughters into responsibility for family work.

While the father was highly revered, the delight and fellowship between father and child was also a pillar of family life. One custom that demonstrated this dynamic was the morning practice of children greeting their father by kissing his hand. They would then stand reverently before him to receive any instruction, or permission to go on their way. At this point, it was also customary for the child to be taken onto the father's lap and embraced.

When you were a child, is that the way you started your day? For most of us, especially as Westerners, it probably wasn't! Our dad may have patted us on the head as we headed out for school, or he may have already left for work. Or maybe dad wasn't there at all for whatever reason. The culture in this nation doesn't typically promote kissing dad's hand first thing in the morning, but the *principles* of love and honor, however demonstrated, are the cornerstone that builds strong families.

Looking to a father for instruction or being lovingly embraced may be foreign to some, but this is the experience Father God wants us to have with Him. He is worthy of absolute reverence, and yet He also delights in our nearness.

The Family Grid

Family dynamics create a "grid" from which a child views life, perceives truth, and learns to relate to God, others, and themselves. A "grid" is a framework—a structure that holds an arrangement of things, or a system, together. Mindsets and belief systems are an arrangement of thoughts held together as a point of reference (a framework) from which we operate.

Your internal grid, as mine, too, began forming while we were still in our mother's womb. Even scientific evidence shows that sounds, words, moods and chemical emotions of a mother affects an unborn child's perceptual and emotional development. Once born, our family structure of father-mother-child continued to shape our point of reference from which we have learned to reason and relate to the myriad issues of life and relationships. Childhood experiences and personal response systems, both good and bad, have all played a part to establish thinking patterns and belief systems, which, in turn, influence our direction and choice.

The family structure was the first and most important earthly foundation created by God for us. **The family unit was designed to be the basis from which we, as children, would learn to relate to all things through a framework of love and honor.** A community of love and honor makes a child grow-up feeling communicated with, connected, and safe. The family unit was designed to be the springboard of identity through honor and responsibility.

Each member of the family is designed to contribute a particular dynamic needed for the healthy growth of those born (or brought) into the family.[2]

- **Dads provide**: identity, safety, and provision
- **Mothers provide**: nurturing, comfort, and guidance
- **Siblings provide**: participation and friendship

Father	Mother	Sibling
Identity	Nurturing	Participation
Safety	Comfort	Friendship
Provision	Guidance	Help

Fathers establish identity through their *name* which all family members share. His name is the "trademark" that says who the child is *connected* to and contains a history for the child regarding where they came from. As the shelter-provider, a father creates an ambient of feeling *safe;* as the food-supplier he creates an ambient of feeling *satisfied*; as the counsel-giver and loving disciplinarian he creates an ambient of *order and direction;* and as supreme ruler, he provides a role model of how to *govern*. His love calls out the destiny in his children.

The mother's role works in *unity with the father*. Through her love the home becomes *fruitful* and *increases*. As she uses her *gifts* in the home and business, she helps to model for the children the importance of developing their gifts (Prov. 31). Moms minister *encouragement, comfort*, and *help*. She *teaches* the children to honor the father and *actively engage* responsibility and accountability to him. She addresses the children's heart issues, and her tenderness establishes an ambient of *grace.*

Children also have an important role. Older siblings especially are to be the **right hand** to the parents. They are to help *care* for the younger children just as they have been cared for. They *communicate* the parent's instructions in a way that's understood, and they *model* a lifestyle of honor toward the parents. They are also companions and provide *friendship.* The role of an older sibling is not one of dominance or being bossy, but of loving service. Their friendship creates a safe way for younger children to learn healthy social skills of sharing and relating to others through a network of love and respect.

The original family grid was designed to be a loving community—each one working together with father as the catalyst, mother as the helper and teacher, and the children as the carriers of divine purpose.

Wait! Don't shut this book! While this may be the blueprint of God for our families, it may not be the reality we knew growing up. For many of us, it probably wasn't! The truth is that many families experience some level of disconnection or painful way of relating. Some families experience an extreme amount of it. These injurious ways can result in what we call "family wounds." Family wounds can act like filters on our perception of God, others, and ourselves (which we will look at in the next chapter). Father God wants to heal our heart and give us a *new grid—His grid*. He wants to give us new eyes that see life through His love instead of through the filter of unhealed pain created by family dynamics or other childhood trauma.

The Divine Grid of God

The earthly family grid wasn't just some great idea put in place by God; it was a reflection of the loving community contained within God Himself. In Genesis 1:26, God said, "Let *Us* make man after *Our* own image" (emphasis mine). The *"Us"* is the Father, Son, and Holy Spirit. God is a One, yet He is Three in One. As man was created in God's image, this means that the Father, Son and Holy Spirit is the divine framework from which we are to live. We were created for "community" (fellowship) with God even as God Himself is in "community".

Living from the grid of relationship with God we experience:

- **The Father:** who gives us identity, safety, and provision
- **The Holy Spirit:** who teaches, guides, and gives comfort
- **The Son:** who shares with us as our Elder Brother and is our Friend

Father	**Son**	**Holy Spirit**
Royal Identity	Protective Elder Brother	Loving Guidance
Safety in His Name	True Friend—Shares Plans	Teaches Truth
Unlimited Provision	Shares Inheritance	Abiding Helper

This grid of the Father, Son, and Holy Spirit is the point of reference from which we are to live: drawing understanding and identity as we relate to God, others and ourselves through a framework of divine love and honor. *The very spirit of community cuts to the heart of independence.*

While the Holy Trinity is best understood through the metaphor of the family grid, the earthly picture is *not* a perfect metaphor: it is *not* to say that the Holy Spirit is female, nor is He the wife of the Heavenly Father, nor is the Son of God the "offspring" of the Father and the Holy Spirit. But the family picture *does* provide for us an understanding of the inherent unity of God as Father, Son, and Holy Spirit and how we relate to God as sons and daughters.

Each person of the Godhead is *individual* in personality and role, yet *They* are in complete union and operate as a *community of One*. The core-nature of this divine community is love, for God is love (1

John 4:8). God is the pattern and foundation of the earthly family; without His presence we *cannot* love.

The Holy Trinity work together as one heart, mind, and purpose: Father is the *Author* from which all purpose and design flow; the Holy Spirit releases the manifest *power* of God regarding divine purpose and activity; and the Son *performs* divine purpose and activity.

About the Father

Father God gives us our identity. He gave all mankind their identity, whether they recognize it or not. He is the Author of your life and mine and is the source of provision for all living things. In the following chapters, we will be studying myriad aspects of who He is and how we can engage a deeper walk in intimate fellowship with Him as our "*Dad*".

About the Son

Jesus is the Son of God who came as Son of Man as the tangible manifestation of the Father's love. He is the *Glory* and *Expression* of the Father. He is the Prince of Peace who brings us into fellowship with the Father and the Spirit, and whose presence causes us to be in harmony and tune with heaven. He teaches us to be true sons who are pleasing to the Father and to live "*Father-focused*". He is our kind Elder Brother who became like us in order to rescue us—He is well acquainted with our weakness. He is also our Friend who laid down His life to save us from death and our own destruction. We will learn more about Him also in the chapters ahead.

About the Holy Spirit

The Holy Spirit is also part of the Godhead. While some of the characteristics of the Holy Spirit, such as Teacher, Helper and Comforter, may be more typically demonstrated by the female gender, Scripture says that God is *neither* male nor female, and yet, within God is *both* paternal (male) and maternal (female) qualities. Both men *and* women were created in the image of God and carry the nature of God. The Holy Spirit moves through *both* and expresses the heart of God through *both*.

The Holy Spirit is the *Spirit of truth* who proceeds from the Father, and is sent to be our ***Helper, Counselor and Comforter*** (John 14: 16-17; 16:13-14). In Scripture, He has many names; His names describe His nature and the expressed power that He releases into our life. He is also known as the *Spirit of grace* (Heb. 10:29), *Spirit of glory* (1 Pet. 4:14), *Spirit of Jesus Christ* (Phil. 1:19), *Spirit of life* (Rom. 8:2), *Spirit of promise* (Acts 1:4-5), *Spirit of adoption* (Rom. 8:15), *Spirit of holiness* (Rom. 1:4), *Spirit of faith* (2 Cor. 4:13), *Spirit of judgment* and *burning fire* (Isa. 4:4), *Spirit of wisdom* and **understanding, *Spirit of counsel* and *might*,** and the *Spirit of knowledge*, and the *fear of the Lord* (Isa. 11:2).

The abiding presence and power of the Holy Spirit makes us the children of God (John 3:5-6). While Jesus is the *Way* of God and the *Way* to the Father, the Holy Spirit is the One who *empowers* us to walk in the *Way*. The Holy Spirit is our divine Teacher who reveals truth to us. This is an important part of His work with us for without the *revelation* of truth, we would be left to our own methods and means . . . and we know where that has gotten us!

The loving unity of the Godhead is demonstrated throughout Scripture. We see how Father *released* the Holy Spirit and *exalted* the Son, how the Spirit *moved* with Father and *empowered* the Son, and how the Son *glorified* Father through *oneness* with the Spirit to accomplish Father's work. **This heartbeat of love in the community of the Godhead serves as the pattern for earthly families.**

Think about how living from this grid would impact families: fathers would initiate life through love and release their wife into fruitfulness and fulfillment, they would lift their children into success and divine fulfillment, wives would honor their husband and work side-by-side with him to train children for divine purposes, and children would honor their father and mother through loving obedience.

When God is invited into our life, home, business, and sphere of influence, His presence will change the way we operate. When God is our point of reference—our divine Center—He (not the world) is our identity; His plans become our purpose and His words become our nourishment.

The Building Blocks of Family

While the healthy family grid is intended to establish building blocks within a child to enable proper growth in relationships—with God, others, and themselves—man's fall in sin changed man's grid, and thus altered family dynamics.

Many people walk through life with building blocks that are missing or damaged by hurtful family structure. But God has a plan of healing and rebuilding our lives, *and* the life of our family. His plan of healing will change the way we operate internally, and thus how we respond externally. His plan begins with the intimate knowledge of Himself as our "grid" and point of reference in all things. It is a divine plan initiated by Father, activated by the Son's death and resurrection, and empowered in our lives by the presence of the Holy Spirit. In the pages ahead we will learn how to engage this wonderful divine plan of God as our Center—our *"grid"*.

Personal Application:

1. How would you describe your family relationships (dad, mom, siblings) growing up?
2. How would you describe your relationship with the Father, Son, and Holy Spirit?
3. How would you describe your sense of connection with others?
4. How would you describe your ability to be in unity with others?

CHAPTER 2

When Earthly Families Fail

We were designed to grow up in a safe place where love and honor shape us for divine purposes. We all come into this world *expecting* to be received by loving hands that will wisely care for us. How do I know? Just ask any adult still dealing with the painful effects of hands that were *not* loving, or were perhaps absent. And we, too, have acted in unloving ways.

Failures are a part of life. None of us escape them. However, the "*safety*" we look for with family is not necessarily found in the complete absence of conflict, but in the *way* that love and honor are *expressed* to one another as we work through issues. It is the *unwillingness* to acknowledge wrongs, the *neglect* of making things right and extending forgiveness, and the *failure* to pursue love that *honors others* that wounds family unity most.

Unloving actions expressed within a family through hurtful words, favoritism, rejection, neglect, anger, and abuse can leave bruised imprints on our hearts and minds. These bruises tell us that we can't always trust others and so we learn to live disconnected and guarded. Other people outside the family also impact our life, but no matter who the perpetrator of harm has been, as children, our bottom-line is most often: *where was dad?* He, after all, was supposed to be our protector.

Most of us have asked that same question (whether consciously or subconsciously), if not with our earthly dad, perhaps with Father God: *"Where were You?"* A father, as the ultimate authority, is also the ultimate one we look to for help and responsibility for our care. We look to him for protection and safety. Because the family grid was created to teach us a healthy perspective of God's own involvement with us, hurtful family dynamics can bruise the way we perceive God and His care. It can even bruise the way we see ourselves and life in general.

Wounds from another's failure can create perceptions most often reflected as: God is distant, no one cares, and I'm worthless. Wounds of the heart become the soil for Satan to plant and water these seeds of thought. Seeds of resentment can grow inside us; we may even blame Father God (again, consciously or subconsciously) for what we perceive to be as His absence, lack of protection, or seeming indifference. While, through training, we may recognize our need to forgive others who harm us, issues with God (or ourselves), may still lie hidden beneath the surface of our thoughts.

God's design was that every generation would be fathered in such a way that each child would learn to relate to Him, others, and to themselves from a framework of divine love: loving and being loved. But when man fell through sin—choosing self-will over God's will—his spirit died. His core-value then changed from the love of God to the love of *self*.

Man's *disconnection* from God created a new point of reference for him . . . himself. In the new grid of *self*-identity, fulfillment for needs was then pursued by leaning on one's *own* understanding.

This grid causes response systems within relationships to function with a focus on our own desires rather than the love of God.

Me	Myself	I
creates own identity	isolation	self-led
security in things /others	self-protection	self-counsel
works to meet own needs	independent	self-help

The framework of "self-centeredness" promotes:

- Self-gratification
- Fear and Blame
- Ignoring God-given responsibility
- Selfish ambition that gives place to *every evil thing* (James 3:16)

Since the fall of man, every one of us is born into a self-centered world with a self-centered nature—a *sin-nature* that is absent of God's glory (Rom. 3:23). The word *"sin"* (Grk. *"hamartia"*) has a number of meanings including: to *be outside* of fellowship, to *wander* from honor, to *violate* God's law, and to err and *miss the target*. What is the *"target"*? The target for mankind is the glory of God contained in the fellowship of divine love. Love brings us into community and is expressed through honor of God and one another. Love upholds the Father's instructions. His commandment to man is simple: love God, others, and ourselves (Matt. 22:37). Love is the core-value of all God's law and instruction.

We all long for love because we were created for love, but sin causes us to fall short of love, and thus of glory. We fall short and others fall short. This falling short causes us to try and fill the void we feel through our own means and methods. **Within the setting of a fallen world, our *expectations* of being *perfectly loved* can never be *fully* met by anyone but God who *is* Love.** His love never fails. And yet, even God's perfect love doesn't always *prevent* painful things from happening. However, His love does provide healing for our heart as His presence mends our brokenness. His Word affirms us and His counsel fills us with peace. His truth teaches us to overcome and to love Him, others and ourselves through intimate fellowship with Him—the Father, Son, and Holy Spirit.

When broken expectations or ill-treatment from another is filtered through our own self-exalting nature, our soul can easily become the spawning ground of resentment and negative thinking. Wounds are the devil's playground. He likes to sow and foster lies in our minds about who we are, who God is, how others relate to us, and how we relate to them. When something negative happens (or is *perceived* as negative), how do we relate to the situation? How do we relate to others involved? How do we relate to God? How do we relate to ourselves?

Ungodly Judgments and Vows

Painful circumstances bring to the surface what is in us and the framework that is directing our thoughts. A framework rooted in the self-life will promote a false means of self-protection through blame, judgments, and vows. Judgments keep us in the cycle of pain. For judgments against others to be true we would have to know *all* things, including another's motives and framework. But we don't. We don't even know the depths of our *own* soul! Only God does. So He says to leave judgment to Him. That may be easier said than done, but for healing in our life to happen, we must let go of judgments against those who have hurt us—both real and perceived hurts. We must also renounce ungodly vows that may have accompanied those judgments.

Ungodly judgments and vows are accusations rooted in condemnation of another. These may be expressed as: *"My father was mean and unfair—I'll never be like him,"* or *"That leader hurt me—I'll never trust authority again,"* or *"People always hurt others—I'll never be close to anyone again."* We even make ungodly vows about God like, *"You didn't stop that from happening—I'll never trust You again."* Such declarations, even unspoken, keep *us* imprisoned.

Strongholds

Satan exploits wounds by speaking lies in *vulnerable* moments to form strongholds in our thinking. A stronghold is a network of internal lies initiated through external circumstances, but *promoted by our agreement.* Scripture says that Satan is the father of lies and is a murderer from the beginning (John 8:44). Lies create a point of reference that is devoid of God's truth and love, and is a place from which the natural mind draws thoughts and makes choices. Living from that counterfeit framework is what devastates our life. Ungodly thinking destroys individuals and families, and thus *destinies*. That is why God desires truth to be in our inward man (Ps. 51:6).

As children, we tend to forgive easily, hope expectantly, and trust blindly. We begin life thinking, "Surely, I am worthy to be loved!" But when offenses are repeated and wounds go unhealed, feelings of disconnection can invade the soul and create a darkened sense of personal worth. Insecurity and rejection can filter our thinking. We may even interpret unhealthy family dynamics as the way God must think about us. Means and methods promoted by the spirit of the world, the flesh, and the devil are then adopted to fill our unmet needs.

By the time we are adults we may have repressed or even forgotten hurtful things that happened. We move on—but not really. Strongholds and lies that entered through wounds may still be secretly operating. The power of ungodly judgments and vows, too, remain operative until they are recognized and renounced. Strongholds and wrong thinking patterns show up in the difficulties we have in rightly relating to circumstances, people, spouses, and authorities, including God. We may flounder through painful mistakes and failures, or we may outwardly appear successful while inwardly feeling constant defeat.

Bitterness is a Pit of Darkness

As a teenager I was angry, rebellious, and at one point tried to take my life. And incredibly, I didn't know "why"! It's amazing how much we can be in pain and not always know the reason or root of our issue. It's like having an infection. You don't always know where the problem is, but you feel the fever that rages in your body. During that time, a pastor asked me if family issues were the cause. I said no, knowing that no family was perfect and that my parents were good Christians. All I knew was that I was miserable inside.

I hated myself and tried to escape the darkness I felt through drugs and alcohol. But the more I "escaped," the darkness grew. I knew my actions were wrong, and felt my problems were simply a deep failure on my part. But I didn't know how to change. I didn't know why I felt so "driven".

What I didn't realize was that hurts I had experienced when younger had been secretly laying a network of wrong thinking— strongholds that I was nurturing through bitterness, self-pity, and rebellion. I was mad at the world because I felt worthless, although I couldn't articulate that at the time. Isn't it strange how we can hurt inside and get mad at everyone one else? Hurting people hurt people because they don't know what to do with their pain. They may not even be able to say why they are mad. I couldn't. I didn't know.

It takes the light of the Holy Spirit to uncover the lies that Satan whispers in our ear that we have believed as truth, but are not. Satan can twist even the most perfect circumstance. Again, look at the Garden of Eden. Satan especially uses negative circumstances and events as an open door to gain an influence into our thought life. While demonic presence uses lies (like a rider on a horse) to enter and oppress our mind, *the root of our pain is our agreement with the lie.* I realize this is a big subject in the area of inner healing, but suffice it to say here, we cannot change our past, but we can change our present—and thus our future—as the Holy Spirit teaches us to identify strongholds and tear them down (2 Cor. 10:4-5). **Remember, ungodly thinking destroys divine destiny; right thinking builds destiny.**

Thanks to a praying mom and dad, when I was twenty the Lord opened the door for me to go to Argentina and be under the ministry of Dr. R. Edward and Eleanor Miller and their son, John, and his wife, Peachy. The well of revival was open and the light of God's glory captivated my heart. There God began a complete stripping of every false thing I had trusted and clung to. God's love didn't leave one dark rock unturned. I found that His light does so many things;

it draws you and creates desire to see Him as He is. You want to know Him intimately. Yet at the same time, you see yourself—your sin and what is contrary to His nature. **In His light you see things as they really are, but you're not afraid—you just desperately want to be clean from the sin that you see so you can be like Him in His holiness.** You are no longer concerned about another's sin—you see the evil of your own *"stuff"* and you want to be free of it.

I saw how hard my heart had become. I saw the pride and agreement with self-centeredness. I saw the darkness I had embraced and I began to hate it; I longed for His righteousness. Only when we see evil for what it is and hate it will we let go of it. In love, God took me by the hand and led me to the cross. There He washed me in the fountain of His precious blood. God's truth and love make us want to run to Him, not away from Him! We see His beauty and no matter what we've done, He invites us to come and be like Him.

So I ran to Him, but my running was a journey. The chains clung tightly to my legs and freedom did not come instantly. But God gave me a promise that if I sought Him, I would find Him when I sought Him with *all my heart* (Jer. 29:13). He wanted my heart . . . all of it. So I set my eyes on Him and pressed in to Him with all I knew how.

The first few months I felt so empty and deeply lost in the pit that my bitterness had created. I couldn't feel the presence of God that I saw others experiencing. That is what bitterness and pride do—they hinder fellowship with Light. I wanted to touch Him, but there was a veil that kept me from entering the glory I saw on other's faces.

One night, during the student's chapel service at the Bible School where I lived, the pastor had the students surround me to intercede for a needed breakthrough. That day had been a particularly difficult one with some areas in my life I had been battling. As they prayed, the lights suddenly went out, but only in that room. The darkness was *unnaturally* thick. Everyone felt it. The prayers grew in intensity—they knew they were fighting for my life. How important is our support and encouragement of one another in life's battles.

A small breakthrough happened that evening as I declared, *"I break agreement with darkness! I yield myself to You, Lord!"* After that night, I found a new freedom in prayer and ability to read the

Word which I hadn't had in a long time. I began to spend as much time in prayer and Scripture as I could. My lame feet were beginning to move. Every time there was a service I was there. I was desperate. I had to find Him. I didn't want just a "touch"; I wanted transformation. I wanted to walk with God. I wanted to know His *abiding* glory. As the months passed, I cultivated a deep personal dependence on the work and presence of the Holy Spirit. As I did, brokenness came. Humility came.

Tears of repentance became my food day and night as the Spirit of truth exposed my rebellion for what it was. The faces of rebellion are many, including apathy. He showed me where self was enthroned and how I thought and acted apart from love, convicting me of disobedience. My prison of darkness was shattering.

The Spirit of understanding invaded my ignorance and His counsel rent the veil of deception that had clouded my thinking. **I heard His voice calling me to come and know His glory, but I knew I couldn't have my ways *and* His glory.** I had to choose. He was giving me an "informed" choice. Agreement with lies had blinded me, but Father was now showing me the *glory* I was created to experience through a life surrendered to Him.

God's love and truth washed away the years of sin and bitterness. And one day—a moment I'll never forget—my chains fell off. I heard them fall. I was free. That moment came during a worship service. The Lord had spoken to me before the service that I was to open my heart and just love Him. As we were singing, I expressed my gratitude for all He had ever done for me. And then I saw Him. I saw Jesus. I was in His presence and my chains fell off. His beauty opened my heart and His presence healed me. There, He gave me a new framework—the framework of intimate fellowship with Him. I now see life with God as my foundation of thought and perspective.

What We Believe Shapes Our Life

Life transformation and healing comes by turning from the love of self and embracing the love of God. As a child, I interpreted others' actions toward me as saying, "You are worthless." I embraced a felt opinion that was not rooted in love. And I, in turn, responded unlovingly. We can never prevent the unloving opinions or actions of another, but our heart *can* be rooted in the embrace of One who *is* Love.

While family dynamics contribute to shaping how we view ourselves, others, and God, the truth is we cannot prevent another's actions, nor blame them for our own internal responses and perceptions. We cannot blame them for the lies that Satan, *and our flesh*, speak to us which we choose to believe. *It is what we believe that shapes our framework*. The place that needs healing is not the circumstance itself, but is within *us*. God heals every *heart* wound through His love and truth. Truth and love tear down ungodly speculations, imaginations and mindsets in order to bring us back into fellowship with God. **The love of God isn't just tender, it is also *violent*. Truth and love tear away every veil so we can see Him with unveiled eyes.** This is key to our wholeness, for we become like Him as we *behold* Him (2 Cor. 3:18).

If we gaze on the darkness of some offense, that is what we become filled with. God wants our gaze on Him. Not long ago, as I was in prayer, I remembered when I was about four years old sitting on my father's lap and looking up into his eyes saying, "Daddy, I just don't know what to do." Circumstances were pressing my little mind and I needed dad to tell me how to deal with life. God, too, is a Father who wants us to feel His embrace as we ask for His counsel regarding the daily events of life.

God's restoration and building in our life is a continual work; He sees what we cannot see. Life with Him is a rich journey of ever *unfolding revelation* of Himself and who we are in Him. Each revelation of God is a catalyst of truth that launches us into deeper realms of freedom that flow with power to live as His beloved child.

As little children longing for love, we have sought approval from those around us. But when faced with loveless actions, we become confused and do not discern the secret lies forming within us. We disconnect and repress the realities that we have no answer for. We escape reality because we don't know how to face it. No one has taught us how to climb onto Father God's lap. We wall our hearts to escape the pain, not realizing we are actually walling *in* the pain.

We don't know how to open our heart to God so we look for love through any means we think will meet our unmet needs. However, when we enter fellowship with God who is love, this will change.

A Parent's Grid

Children are vulnerable and are not born with systems of protection. They are dependent on another's care for them. But sometimes the one caring for them is operating out of their own unhealed wounds. A parent's own response system is influenced by their own early family dynamics. Their point of reference has also been shaped by personal experiences (good and bad), role models (good and bad), and types of support systems (or lack of them). They, like we, are also influenced by the spirit realm (good and bad). Many of our parents are on their own journey of being healed. Some have walked in wholeness all their life. And some are still lost at sea waiting to be rescued.

Unmet needs can be expressed in many ways, including depression, anger, anxiety, isolation, and rebellion. It is also expressed through addictions. In truth, the list is endless. While family wounds can leave us with a deep sense of unmet need, there are other harmful influences that also shape our thinking. These include culture and customs that work to destroy a healthy family unit. In some nations boys are esteemed and girls are not, women are shrouded, and fathers sell their children to sex slave-traders. Other cultures allow the killing of unwanted baby girls as an accepted practice. Societies that practice abortion promote a cultural mindset that tolerates the destruction of another's life for self-seeking purposes. Much of our Western culture media promotes anti-family behavior through acts of dishonor portrayed in children to parents, parents to children, and spouse to spouse.

A child's thinking can be influenced by *many* sources including a child's own *mis*perceptions. Even the best parental skill cannot always prevent negative things from happening to a child, nor control a child's internal perceptions. Generational curses, too, are another influence that can be at work in a life—an influence that many may not be aware of. While all curses are broken at the cross, continued personal sin can give place to curses to operate that influence thinking habits and choices.

When Fathers Are Absent

It is a proven fact that strong fathering helps children do better in school, are more confident, are less likely to be depressed, and are more successful in relationships. Studies show that fathers who are involved with their children provide practical support and serve as models for their children's development. In the natural, some may think it's primarily the son who needs a father to guide and instruct him. But a daughter needs a father just as a son does. She needs a father who will teach her and give her a visual role model of what a righteous man is, and how she ought to keep herself pure for marriage. A father prepares both a son and daughter for success in life.

Studies reveal that children of fatherless families have greater tendency toward early sexual activity, mental illness, anxiety, poor educational performance, and increased demonstration of aggressive, uncooperative or antisocial behavior. They are also more likely to suffer child abuse or early death.[1] **Please note, however, these are just statistics and do not define a person's behavior just because a father may not be present for any number of reasons.**

According to US data, the presence of fathers has significant impact in the home, and so does their absence:

- 85% of all children that exhibit behavioral disorders come from fatherless homes. (Source: Center for Disease Control)
- 90% of all homeless and runaway children are from fatherless homes. (Source: *U.S. D.H.H.S.*, Bureau of the Census)
- 71% of all high school dropouts come from fatherless homes. (Source: National Principals Association Report on the State of High Schools.)
- 75% of all adolescent patients in chemical abuse centers come from fatherless homes. (Source: *Rainbows for all God's Children.*)
- 63% of youth suicides are from fatherless homes. (Source: *U.S. D.H.H.S.*, Bureau of the Census)

- 80% of rapists motivated with displaced anger come from fatherless homes. (Source: Criminal Justice & Behavior, Vol. 14, p. 403-26, 1978)
- 70% of juveniles in state-operated institutions come from fatherless homes. (Source: U.S. Dept. of Justice, *Special Report*, Sept 1988)
- 85% of all youths sitting in prisons grew up in a fatherless home. (Source: *Fulton Co. Georgia Jail Populations*, Texas Dept. of Corrections 1992)
- 71% of teenage pregnancies are to children of single parents. (U.S. Dept. of Health)
- The U.S. Department of Health and Human Services states that there were more than 1,000,000 documented child abuse cases in 1990. In 1983, it found that 60% of perpetrators were women with sole custody. Shared parenting can significantly reduce the stress associated with sole custody, and reduce the isolation of children in abusive situations by allowing both parents' to monitor the children's health and welfare and to protect them.
- "The National Fatherhood Institute reports that 18 million children live in single-parent homes. Nearly 75% of American children living in single-parent families will experience poverty before they turn 11. Only 20% in two-parent families will experience poverty." (Melinda Sacks, "*Fatherhood in the 90's: Kids of Absent Fathers More "at risk",*" San Jose Mercury News, 10/29/95)
- "The feminization of poverty is linked to the feminization of custody, as well as linked to lower earnings for women. Greater opportunity for education and jobs through shared parenting can help break the cycle." (David Levy, Ed., *The Best Parent is Both Parents*, 1993)
- Fathers are more likely to be the protector of the child: a British study found that children are 33 times more likely to be abused by a live-in boyfriend or stepfather. (www.canadiancrc.com. "*Fatherlessness in Canada*". July 1, 2008)

These statistics translate to mean that children from a fatherless home are:

- 5 times more likely to commit suicide.
- 32 times more likely to run away.
- 20 times more likely to have behavioral disorders.
- 14 times more likely to commit rape.
- 9 times more likely to drop out of high school.
- 10 times more likely to abuse chemical substances.
- 9 times more likely to end up in a state-operated institution.
- 20 times more likely to end up in prison.

Many say that in America we are living in a "fatherless" generation. Fatherlessness is expressed not only as the absence of a father, but when a father who is present does not, or *cannot*, provide for, or guide a child, whether through ignorance, inability, or even illness. Reasons for fatherlessness include: death, job situation, divorce, lack of commitment, believing that children are the "wife's responsibility," priority on materialism, drug use, affairs, rejection of conventional roles, and a parent's personal problems. Nonresident dads may keep involved in their children's lives, but often end up in a role more as a close relative rather than a father giving guidance and counsel. All these can greatly impact a child's full emotional growth.

Fatherlessness can also be a "self-inflicted" plight . . . a choice. Some people *reject* their parents and authorities. In the 1960s, America experienced a whole generation that rejected fathers both at home and in society. The rejection was also expressed by the removing of prayer and God's Word from public education and other settings. At the same time, the teaching of evolution was implemented. Evolution is the rejection of God's fatherhood. It is man's attempt to deny that our life came from Him—thus we don't have to answer to Him for what we do with it. But we do.

I currently know of two precious young men who are classic cases of the statistics on fatherlessness just mentioned. Both are in their mid-twenties and are sitting in jail. They did not spend much time with their biological father while growing up because the parents had divorced and the father was in prison. The stepfather, who raised them, committed suicide ... one of the boys found his body. What shall we do with the fatherless who are crying for a father?

People need fathers. People need Father God. Our wholeness and destiny depends on His presence, but we must realize that Father God never left us—we left Him. And yet, He calls each one of us to turn with our whole heart to Him and be fathered by His wise and loving care. As we do, we will, in turn, learn to father the fatherless.

A New Grid

We are born into a fallen world that operates apart from God. The cross and resurrection of Jesus Christ is the divine gateway through which we return to fellowship with the Father, Son, and Holy Spirit and obtain a *new grid*. From this place of fellowship we are able to draw right conclusions based on divine truth, and healthy perspectives rooted in divine love. God wants our point of reference to be Himself as our Father, the Son as our Elder Brother and King, and the Holy Spirit as our Helper and Teacher of truth. **When God is our point of reference, it will change the way we relate to everyone and everything.**

Jesus, as Son of Man, lived by this grid. He wasn't a stranger to cruel words hurled at Him who was born of a virgin. He wasn't oblivious to His own brother's unbelief. He wasn't removed from the failings of imperfect earthly parents. He wasn't unmoved by the passing of Joseph while still a young man. He wasn't sheltered from temptation nor hidden from the hostility of men. He was touched by our infirmities, yet without sin for He lived rooted in the love of Abba, and walked immersed in the presence of the Holy Spirit, yielding always to God's leading and desires.

God offers to us the same grid that Jesus had. We *can* walk in wholeness. We come as children, just as we are, to Jesus. Jesus takes us to Father. We ask Him for truth to identify lies and strongholds that have held us captive in our minds through inward agreement. As the Holy Spirit shows us falsehoods we have embraced, we rend them from us by His power in us and replace them with God's truth.

This path of divine wholeness is the way on which we walk into our full destiny.

God's truth sets us free, but freedom brings change. Some prefer to continue in blame. Disconnecting is sometimes easier than connecting. Sometimes its easier to be angry, kick the dog, yell at our spouse, throw tantrums, hit the kids, buy the bottle, and on, and on. Sometimes we'd rather coddle agreement with an area of "struggle" rather than lose that "friend". Sometimes it's easier to put on a pretty face and say, "Everything is fine," and never let God deal with those wayward areas or touch the broken places within us. But waywardness and denial destroy us.

Father God wants us healed and walking free in the full authority of who we are as His sons and daughters. He wants us to live in the reality of His nearness and the knowledge of our worth and value in His sight. His grid helps us see Him as safe and involved, and not as how our earthly father may have been. It enables us to trust the leading of the Holy Spirit with confidence that He is not irrational or controlling as perhaps a mother may have been. God's grid unveils our eyes to see Jesus as Lord and Savior *and* as a loving Elder Brother—not as how an earthly brother may have treated us. God's grid teaches us to engage with Him in the midst of life's struggles as our Father, Counselor, and Helper. It enables us to see others and ourselves through the lenses of perfect love and divine purpose. **Living within the framework of the community of God we know we are loved, and we love.**

Whether the family dynamics in which we grew up were wonderful, terrible, or somewhere in-between, the Holy Spirit will show us where our thoughts are operating from a wrong point of reference, thus hindering success and relationship with God, others, or ourselves. The Father of all fathers invites us with open arms to come and live from His framework. He has an abundant supply for all we need, including all unmet needs lingering from childhood.

Reaching out to meet our unmet needs through a framework of self only perpetuates the pain that compels our reach. Just as children need wholesome touch and healthy nurturing, as God's children, we, too, need His touch and nurturing words. Father God knows our need *and* our destiny. He wants to father us both for wholeness *and* the eternal purpose for which we have been born by His Spirit. He calls us daily to engage in a life rooted in the fellowship of His unfaltering love.

Personal Application:

1. What was your parent's personal grid like?
2. How do you view yourself? Valuable? Wanted? Loved? Loving?
3. Do you see any stronghold or wrong agreement in your life?
4. Have you made any judgment or vow regarding another person?

CHAPTER 3

Healing Family Wounds

"When my father and my mother forsake me,
then the LORD will take me up."
Psalm 27:10

Though family may sometimes fail us, and we them, God never fails us. He wants to stop the pain *and* the darkness that promotes continued affliction. Some wounds go very deep and the crippling effect can last a lifetime if not addressed. Some people "stuff" the pain of past events while others build walls or hide in addictions. Others find help. Not dealing with lingering issues only holds us captive to the pain and the past.

The evidence of unhealed pain reminds me of America's naval ship, the *U.S.S. Arizona,* that lies at the bottom of Pearl Harbor in Oahu, Hawaii. The U.S. battleship was sunk in the infamous Japanese Naval attack in December, 1941. Today, oil within the ship continues to seep in tiny quantities that rise to the surface of the harbor where the ship lies. They call these seepages the "tears" of the 1177 men who died inside the *Arizona*'s sunken hull. The "tears" of oil are the evidence of what is still trapped beneath.

What rises to the top of our thoughts and emotions in stressful circumstances? Do we have "buttons" that get pushed? Are there unresolved issues that linger beneath the surface of routine life? Unhealed pain *will* come out in one way or another whether through troubled relationships, inability to draw near to God, guilt and shame, or feeling "unworthy". Our "tears" may rise as anxiety or anger, or perhaps in conversation as a simple comment, but one that carries a resentful edge.

Unloving actions can never be justified, but neither can our remaining in the lies or bitterness inspired by those actions. If we stay captive to the past, we will not move forward into the full purposes that Father God has uniquely designed for our life. Time is short and our life too valuable to waste in the failures of yesterday—ours or anybody else's. **We can't change the past or what other people choose to say and do. We can only change *us* by coming to the Great Physician's healing room—the cross.**

The cross breaks the tyranny of lies and the mind of the flesh that engages them. Only when our carnal man with its natural understanding is buried with Christ, can we be released into a new life of triumph by the Spirit. For this to happen, *I* must be crucified (Gal. 2:20).

At the cross we find healing as we come to truth, extend forgiveness, embrace the way of love, and engage a lifestyle of honor.

1 Healing Through Truth

> Jesus said, "... I am the way, and the truth, and the life;
> no one comes to the Father but through Me." (John 14:6)

Our freedom and healing was won at the cross by Jesus; He is the *door of truth* that opens into Father's healing room (John 10:9). The lies we've believed have kept us outside while our hand has covered our wound in an attempt to heal it. But it hasn't. Healing requires us to come out of hiding, denial, and pretending, and be honest about our own heart, thoughts, and actions. As we dare to come to the Father, we come as a child presenting our heart to Him, asking Him to remove the thorn that pierced it and cleanse the present infection. Father bends tenderly over us and uses His *right hand of truth* to remove the thorny lie (Ps. 20:6; 21:8). Jesus is the Father's right hand. He Himself wore the *crown of thorns* that has held our mind as prisoners to the curse of fallen mindsets. The bleeding hands, feet, and side of Incarnate Truth exposed and condemned the vile lie that we are unloved.

God's truth is the healing antidote to the paralyzing poison of the devil's deceptions. Satan has employed *falsehood* to rob us of love, power, and a sound mind, and *sin* as a weapon to destroy intimacy with God. His lies have worked to kill the delight of who we are as precious and valuable, and hinder our engagement with divine purpose. Like a snake, Satan's cunning words have sought our agreement in order to sever our embrace with the Word of God and cut off our destiny. The framework of self has glued our eyes to the failure of others and things we cannot change, drawing our thoughts to rehearse any personal loss that has been incurred. But this ungodly gaze ignores God and neglects the state of our own heart. **Truth has come to return our gaze to God and make our heart right.**

Jesus said that as we *abide in truth*, the truth would set us free (John 8:31-32). **Truth magnifies God as greater than man and circumstances.** It sees His love and hears His counsel in the midst of our tragedies. Lies lead us into self-destructive ways, but truth leads us into life and liberty. Truth is found in *fellowship* with God and His Word (John 17:17). It is revealed to our spirit and understanding by the Holy Spirit. God is truth and His people are called to be a people of truth (Zech. 8:3).

At the cross, the stream of Jesus' blood flowed to wash away our pain and sorrow, as well as the false grid that makes us feel justified with our own sin. Truth gives us *divine* perspective (versus human reasoning). Truth unveils the face of God as Holy Love that causes us to see ourselves as His beloved. It causes us to also see others in the light of His goodness—including those who have hurt us.

Truth restores us to right thinking. When we believe the truth that God is near, that is how we'll respond to life. If we believe we need *His* approval alone, we won't drown in the rejection of others. If we believe He has a divine plan for our lives, we won't try to figure things out on our own. If we believe He loves mankind that is how we'll perceive others. **And if we believe we are His beloved and are *not* "abusable," we will live with authority and right boundaries.**

We must come to the cross in humility on bended knee, asking God to search our hearts to see what hurtful ways are in us (Ps. 139:23-24). The stiff neck of pride rejects the cross because the cross requires the laying down of self—the same self that from the beginning was filled with pride as it said, "*I* know better than God." But Jesus said that His sheep *hear* His voice and humbly *follow* Him (John 10:27). As He leads us to resurrection life through the way of the cross, we learn to recognize lies and sin in the light of truth, and renounce them. This brings healing.

2   Healing Through Forgiveness

The *natural* response of fallen man is to hurt those who hurt us. The carnal mind wants retribution, revenge, and justice. What they did was unfair, unkind, insensitive, and cruel. We want them to pay for how they've hurt us. We want them to feel sorry for what they've done and the pain they've inflicted on us through their actions, or through their absence.

The fundamental nature of an offense is rooted in a broken law of love. A broken law demands justice. However, vengeful and self-centered responses on our part can never repair what was broken. We cannot change the past, nor can justice be served on the platter of unforgiveness. God is a just God, but His ways are not our ways. He loves justice and *will* make all things right in His time and His way. He does not approve of wrong actions, but to heal us, He *requires* us to forgive others just as He has forgiven us. This is *right action* in His eyes. In fact, we *must* forgive others to receive His forgiveness.

Jesus taught four important principles regarding forgiveness:

- Forgiveness is released to us ***when*** we forgive those who sin against us (Matt. 6:12)

- If we do not forgive others, Father will not forgive us (Matt. 6:15)
- We are judged in the same way we judge others (Matt. 7:2)
- We are to forgive unconditionally (Matt. 18:22)

Unforgiveness is a place of torment—not for the other person—but for us. When we continually replay the events of the past and meditate on resentment, we hold *ourselves* captive to the past. When we deliberately ignore someone and think about how we can withhold good things from them, we are inviting darkness to dwell in us. Bitterness in the heart distorts our perception of everything and causes us to see the world—past, present, and future—through a dark filter of personal woe. God created us to live in joyful expectation, not woe. Woe is self-focused.

Some people forgive readily, others with difficulty—perhaps because of the nature of the offense (or offenses), or the depth of grief involved. Some say it is impossible and the offense unforgiveable. But our healing *cannot* come until we are willing to give up ***our control*** of circumstances *and* others and forgive those who have hurt us.

Unforgiveness is a lie that makes us feel we have a special power over the other person, but in reality, it drains us of power as it eats away joy and hinders fellowship with God. Unforgiveness holds our emotions in a snare of ceaseless grief. It pillages the peace of our soul over things we cannot change, and holds us captive in a loveless place.

That family member who broke the law of love did so because of a multitude of reasons. We may never know the depths of why, but Father God does. Every one of us can be so lost in our own world of pain and unmet needs that we don't realize the hurt we *commit*, or love we *omit*. The ones who have hurt us may not know, or unfortunately, may not care—or have the capacity to care. But God cares, and the bottom line is that we live our life before Him, in Him, and through Him. Only when we give the situation to Him can healing flood our heart where earthly families fail.

To drink the cup of God's healing waters our hand must let go of the offense. As we do, our hand is free to grasp Father's hand that pulls us up onto His lap, and into His caring arms. There He imparts the love and value that our family was unable to give us. His love heals the *root* of our pain while removing any feeling in us of inferiority or shame.

Forgiving others opens the portal of God's forgiveness toward us so that we can ***experience*** His nearness; His nearness ministers to our *deepest* need. Forgiveness brings closure to the open-ended cycle of inward suffering as we release that individual into the Father's hands. As Son of Man, Jesus was unmercifully beaten and crucified, yet He forgave those who beat Him. He didn't wait for them to ask His forgiveness for what they were doing; He didn't wait for them to say, "I'm sorry." He said, *"Father, forgive them, for they know not what they do"* (Luke 23:34). Only when we give ourselves to divine love can we have such a perspective when others act cruelly.

Such love shows that we are to forgive others of their *loveless* crimes. Jesus was not *above* the pain of the cross. He felt it all—outwardly and inwardly. Not only was His body beaten, but He experienced the download of *all* the sin and infirmity of *all* mankind upon Himself, including yours and mine. Think about that for a moment. Jesus experienced every hurt we have ever received *and* the hurt we have inflicted on others, whether through commission or omission. On the cross, He experienced the full cup of our sin; He experienced our dark mindsets and loveless response systems—taking them all upon Himself. He did this to secure forgiveness for us.

And look at what the Father did with Jesus' sacrifice—He turned evil (man's cruel actions) to become a blessing. Jesus' suffering became the payment for our redemption. As He forgave those who nailed Him to the cross, He committed Himself into the hands of the Father. Father God has promised that *all things work together for good to those who love Him and are called according to His purpose* (Rom. 8:28). Anything we have ever gone through and have given into our Heavenly *Papa's* hands, He can turn to be a blessing. **As we commit our lives to God, even the negative events in life can become catalysts of change that move us into greater realms of divine purpose to impact others' lives for good.**

The opposite is true as well: when we do *not* commit ourselves to the Father in the midst of painful circumstances, our own responses can become catalysts of change that *destroy* our life and hurt those around us. I have heard it said more than once that it is not what happens *to* us, but what happens *in* us that shapes our life most.

Stepping Outside the Blame Box

As truth exposes bitter roots, the act of forgiveness *uproots* them from continuing to poison our heart. Forgiveness breaks the controlling mandates of self. When Jesus said to forgive seventy times seven, He didn't mean we are to count the number of offenses, but that we should forgive *always*! Such forgiveness means we take off our "judge's" robe, repent of judgments and vows, and renounce the deception that tells us we have the right to be another's judge and jury. God alone has that place and He says, "*Judge not lest you be judged*" (Matt. 7:1). As we put the offense and offender in Father's hands, our actions are stamped with Father's approval as being pleasing to Him. When we forgive others, we are honoring the Father who tells us to do so.

Another healing aspect of taking responsibility for our own attitudes is that it frees us from living with a "victim" mentality. When finger-pointing is replaced with uplifted hands of worship, power is restored to our life.

We cannot demand accountability of another person; we can only be accountable for our own responses. When we remove our stranglehold from the neck of another, we free Father's hands to deal with them in His time and *His* way. His way always seeks redemption! It is not that we condone a wrongful event, or justify the wrong, but that we put justice in Father's hands. His justice is accurate—ours is not. **Forgiveness chooses to *trust* Father God's leadership in our life as He works all things for good**. Forgiveness chooses to *trust* Father God to work out *His* own plan in another's life.

Walls versus Boundaries

When we feel hurt by others, the natural mind may say, "I'm going to build a wall around me and no one is coming in unless I say so!" We don't trust another's actions and we want protection, so we live guarded to one degree or another. Pain can cause us to pull back or even isolate. But self-protecting walls are self-defeating by nature because they operate by a *spirit of offense* and *fear*. Anything built through agreement with offense and fear will work death in us. There may be times when we *do* need literal protection and we may need to notify an authority. This is not having a "wall," but a right boundary.

Father doesn't want us to have walls of fear, but He does want us to relate to one another with *right boundaries*. Its okay to tell someone "no" when we do not want them to cross lines with us. There are righteous boundaries that *do* need to be established as we walk in love and speak the truth. This promotes inward confidence and better relationships. The important thing to discern is if we are operating in fear, or in truth and love.

Forgiving Ourselves

Family members and others are not the only ones we need to forgive. We must also forgive ourselves. This includes *freeing ourselves* from self-imposed judgments and vows. Self-condemnation is ungodly thinking. We must stop it! It is not love. Satan is the accuser of the brethren and we must not join him to tear ourselves down through self-punishment for past failures. This is not pleasing to God. Keeping ourselves captive in unforgiveness robs us of joy, peace, and strength. This means we are also robbing Father of the delight of having a joyful child around! How can we please Him if we are sad and without love? When God says to forgive, it means forgiving ourselves, too. If He has forgiven us, then choosing to not forgive ourselves is revering our own thinking more than God's thoughts and our judgments greater than His Word.

Letting Go of "Grudges" Against God

Sometimes we carry judgments against God for not preventing harm or not doing what *we* want Him to do. We must also put down our God-blaming stick and let go of grudges against Him. These get us absolutely nowhere, except out of fellowship with the very One we need the most. Grudges are rooted in pride and link with Satan as an accuser. God is Holy and infinite in understanding and how He does things. Some day, when we see Him face to face, we will have the answers to our myriad questions. But until then, a life of wholeness and power is released through honoring and trusting the One who is pure in His love and wisdom. Our tiny mind doesn't have to understand everything, though we'd like it to!

3   Healing Through the Affirmation of Love

Each of us perceives affirmation through specific actions of others—actions that tell us whether we are loved and valued, or not. The way we perceive affirmation is called our *"love language"*. **Wounds are deepest when family wounds impact our specific love language, whether through abuse *or* neglect.** Author Gary Chapman has written a series of books on what he calls man's five "love languages". He lists them as: *words of affirmation, physical touch, quality time, acts of service, and gifts.*[1] There may be more, but these, he says, are the basics.

Knowing we are loved and affirmed is important. Even Abba Father affirmed His Son, Jesus (Matt. 3:17). When our love language is *words of affirmation*, we feel loved by encouraging words. When it is *physical touch*, we feel affirmed through hugs and pats on the back. When our love language is *quality time*, we feel valued when dad or mom takes time with us. And when it is *acts of service*, we feel loved when a parent takes time to help us with things. When our love language is *gifts*, we feel valued when a father gives us something simply because he wants to show us that he cares about us.

Both *abuse* and *neglect* by family in the area of our specific love language also convey a message to us as children—a message that we are *not* loved or valued. Both verbal abuse, as well as the *absence* of encouraging words, can make us feel unloved; physical abuse or the absence of hugs and pats on the back can make us feel unvalued; a parent who is too busy for us can make us feel we are not *worth* their time; a parent who is never there to help us, or never thinks about giving us something just because they want to show their love can make us feel unnoticed or not valued. Giving gifts to manipulate, or to compensate for lack of interaction, is also an abuse of the *"gift"* love language.

Father God made each one of us unique; we perceive (and give) love in specific ways. The sense of being unloved can make us feel depressed and angry and is a root cause of many behavioral issues in children and young people. **If our parent's own love language was abused in their own formative years, without healing, their actions toward us will generally spring from a grid of their own sense of feeling unloved, unvalued, or not validated.** And too, our parent's own love language may be different than our own—their gifts were nice, but our heart was longing for words of affirmation.

A life of power is one that is rooted and grounded in God's love (Eph. 3:17; Rom. 5:5). No matter what our love language is, God manifests His love and affirmation to us in *every possible way*!

- **Words of affirmation**: God affirms us through His Word. Read it! It is full of His passion and affirmation of who we are to Him. We are His beloved. God speaks to us not only through His Word, but through myriad ways including dreams, visions, pictures in our spirit-man, nature, and others. The voice of God is generally heard as an inner voice or "knowing," and His words affirm, encourage, and counsel us with love.
- **Touch**: God touches us through His manifest presence. As we learn to walk with Him, we learn to know and recognize His presence and activity. God also sends people into our lives to minister the tangible touch of His love and care. The ministry of the Body of Christ to one another is the tangible touch of God's love. God can even use a non-believer to touch your life with His blessing. He is not limited.
- **Quality time**: The Father, Son, and Holy Spirit are *always* available for quality time with us. God promised that if we will draw near to Him, He *will* draw near to us (James 4:8). He is always accessible and wants us to come and meet with Him. When we engage in undistracted time with God He will renew our strength, and give us fresh revelation and counsel. He will show us His heart and His plans regarding what He is doing, and how He wants us to participate with Him.
- **Acts of service**: The cross was the greatest act of service ever given. Yet the expression of God's love didn't stop there. He continues to show His love through acts of service in help, guidance, provision, and myriad ways too numerous

to count on a daily basis. Sometimes we just need to stop and thank God for all the things that He *has* done for us, rather than what He *hasn't* done. Thankfulness and praise are the way into His presence! (Ps. 100:4)
- **Gifts**: God lavishes us with gifts. The *greatest* gifts He ever gave us was the gift of His Son and the indwelling presence of His Holy Spirit (John 4:10; Luke 11:13). Gifts from God are expressed in so many ways. Every blessing is a gift. Every talent, ability, and call is a gift not just *to* us, but *through* us to others. The Father, Son, and Holy Spirit each have specific spiritual gifts for us, too. In Romans 12 is a list of gifts from the Father—*prophecy, service, teaching, encouragement, giving, leadership, and the gift of mercy*. In 1 Corinthians 12 is a list of gifts from the Holy Spirit: *word of wisdom, word of knowledge, gift of faith, gifts of healing, miracles, prophecy, discerning of spirits, tongues, and interpretation of tongues.* And in Ephesians 4 is a list of gifts from Jesus: *apostles, prophets, evangelists, pastors and teachers.*

Love Received Must Flow Out

God is able to fill every unmet need; Father knows how to minister to us in every area of our love language. **However, the true healing power of God's love can only be *fully* experienced by *giving* what we receive.** God's love is a river that heals *as* it flows. That is why one of the biggest hindrances to healing is *self-pity*. Self-pity is like a clog in the pipe that stops the flow of life. It is the hand that takes rather than gives. Self-pity *promotes* feelings of being unloved because it is self-seeking; it operates like a "black hole" that absorbs, but does not give. 1 Corinthians 13:5 says that *love is not self-seeking.* When we become God-centered rather than self-centered, then love will flow.

Healing doesn't come by seeking to be loved, *but seeking to love*. When we seek to love others, the movement of God's love through us will automatically make us feel loved, too. Look at the gifts God gives us to express His love—they are given *to* us, but are not *for* us, but for service to others. They are not meant to be self-gratifying, self-promoting, or self-exalting because love is not self-serving. God's gifts are His way of blessing us by blessing others *through* us. Father God wants to not only affirm His love to us, but affirm His love to others through our words and actions. When we *give* His love, we feel full of His love! When we feel His love, we feel whole.

God's Word teaches that the *greatest* pursuit in life should be to love and that without it, we are nothing (1 Cor. 13:1). **To pursue love is to seek His nature to fill our every thought, action, word, and motive in every circumstance.**

"Love is patient, love is kind, and is not jealous;
love does not brag, and is not arrogant, does not act unbecomingly;
it does not seek its own, is not provoked, does not take into
account a wrong suffered, does not rejoice in unrighteousness,
but rejoices with the truth; bears all things, believes all things,
hopes all things, endures all things. Love never fails..."
1 Corinthians 13:4-7

4 Healing Through Honor

Many people do not realize the power of honor, but God says that honor releases the promise of blessing and well-being. Of the Ten Commandments God gave to Moses, the command for children to honor their parents was the only one accompanied by a promise:

"Honor your father and your mother as the Lord your God has commanded you, that your days may be prolonged and that it may go well with you on the land which the Lord your God gives you" (Deut. 5:16).

When we choose to *be* honorable toward parents, we release the promise of God to bless us with well-being and a full destiny. The opposite is also true—*dishonor* of parents reaps destruction and cuts off God's blessing (Deut. 21:20-21). Dishonoring parents makes us dishonorable and provides a place in us for curses to operate

(Prov. 26:2; Deut. 28). A curse causes fruitfulness and wholeness to whither.

The word *"honor"* (Heb. *"kabad"*) means: public esteem, reverence (respect mingled with love and devotion), and recognition of the right of one who has a *superior standing*. Honor is an attitude of esteem accompanied by actions of obedience. This same word *"kabad"* is also used in the Old Testament for *"glory"* — a term used to describe the majestic splendor of God's attributes and presence.

When we respect and revere a father and mother and seek to bring them honor, it forms within us a framework that our life is not about us. Honor is the attitude *and action* of humility that acknowledges someone else as being greater than ourselves. Honor cuts to the heart of self-centeredness because honor involves the laying down of self. Parents, of all people, should be honored because they are the very reason for our own existence. Thus they are *greater than we are*.

When we revere parents and seek to bring them honor (rather than esteeming *ourselves* as greater), the glory of God is released in our lives. Jesus honored His Father and brought Abba glory, rather than glorifying Himself. The cross was the ultimate act of honor as Jesus laid down His own life for the Father's will. That act of honor released healing and divine glory to mankind. To honor the Father's will, we must honor parents and the fathers that God puts in our life. This releases healing and glory in us and in the earth. We honor our parents not because of what they do or don't do, but because of their position. We honor because we choose to be an honorable person. Honoring them honors God.

True honor is motivated by love, not fear. Fear is not of God and causes us to feel *powerless.* **Love and humility *empower* us for right action**; we were created for power — righteous power. Some actions can look honorable, but if our motive is to win man's approval for *personal fulfillment* (rather than to please God), or our actions are motivated by the fear of man, *that* is not honor, nor is it true humility. We must be motivated by love.

I realize that because of a parent's harshness or sin, some would say they cannot honor those who failed them, or weren't there for them. But honor isn't so much about the other person as it is about *our own* attitude. As God's sons and daughters we are to be a people of honor. While our parents are held accountable to God for their actions, we are also held accountable for our own attitudes.

Please understand that honoring parents does *not* mean willing obedience to an activity they may ask or demand of us that is contrary to God's Word. Many lives have been deeply wounded through ungodly activities of parent's demands with vulnerable children. Father God wants to heal those wounds and teach us true honor. Jesus was the most whole person on earth and He lived a lifestyle of honor. He was not a "suck up". He was never intimidated. But He was humble and obedient to God's Word and He lived to glorify Abba Father. God was His grid, not self and not fear.

Jesus' work on the cross broke the power of mankind's self-centered grid as self-exaltation was condemned to death. Now Jesus calls us to pick up our cross and follow Him. Picking up *our* cross means *we* are no longer our point of reference—God is. The "rights" that the flesh demands are buried in the grave. Healing is ours at the cross where we see all things through Father's eyes. We see truth, forgiveness, love, and honor.

Personal Application:

1. Ask Father to search your heart. What does He want you to break agreement with? As He shows you, ask Him to wash you completely. Example: *"Father, show me Your heart, and my own. Show me truth. Father, I acknowledge my sin. I ask You to forgive me of (name sin). I break agreement with it right now. I renounce the lie that (name the lie that you have believed). I break agreement with it and I command every spirit that has come in through that lie and my sin to go now from me. I ask You, Jesus to wash me from all sin and disobedience. I declare the truth that (speak the truth that He shows you). Father, fill me now with Your Holy Spirit as I surrender to You and follow Your leading completely from this day forward."*
2. Ask Father to show you anyone you need to forgive. This includes family members or any other person, **including**

yourself. Verbally declare: *"I forgive _____ (name of individual) for _____ (words / actions). I let the offense go and I release them from all obligation regarding it. Father, I ask that You would cleanse me from all resentment and I ask that You would bless them with the revelation of Yourself, even as You have revealed Yourself to me."* (Read: Matthew 7:1-5, 12; Colossians 3:13; Matthew 18:21-35)

3. Ask Father God to show you any walls you may have and what that wall is. Ask Him to hold you as you give Him permission to take down the false-security around your heart. Ask Him what He is going to replace that wall with and let Him show you or speak to you what it is. You might get a picture, or word, or sense of what that is (example: His arms of love, His shield of favor, or maybe something else).

4. Ask Father what judgment or vow you might have made against a father or mother (Example judgment: "My father didn't love me." Example vow: "I will never be like him." Or example judgment: "My parents were too strict." Example vow: "I will do what I want"). Verbally declare: *"I renounce the unrighteous judgment that my father / mother _____. I renounce the vow that _____. I let the offense go. Jesus, wash away all sin regarding this as I surrender fully to You."* (Read: John 8:15-16; 2 Corinthians 5:10; Romans 14:12-13)

5. Ask Father to fill you with His love as you declare gratitude and praise. Example: *"Father, fill me with Your awesome love! As You wash away all guilt and shame, replace them with peace and glory. I embrace Your wisdom and grace over my life. I declare that I no longer have a spirit of fear, but I have a Spirit of love, power and a sound mind. I thank You that I am now filled with strength, hope, and courage as I yield to Your Spirit of holiness to change me. I thank You that I am blessed as I embrace a lifestyle of honor and humility. I discern Your love for me, Father. Your goodness is with me continually. My heart will run after You that I might know You intimately. In Jesus' name, Amen."*

CHAPTER 4

You Can Call Him *"PAPA"*

"For you have not received the spirit of bondage again to fear;
But you have received the Spirit of adoption,
Whereby we cry, 'Abba, Father.'"
Romans 8:15

Healing of the wounded heart frees us to reach out and receive all that Father God has for us. If we relate to God from a painful grid of how earthly fathers or authority figures interacted with us, it can place blocks and filters on the way we interact with Him as our Father. That is a problem, for the very heart and nature of God is that of a Father... a good, near, and personal Father. Salvation through the Son and the abiding presence of the Holy Spirit were sent from the Father. Everything we need comes from our Father.

Because of negative experiences with earthly fathers or leaders, we may have a poor concept of what true fathering looks like. Worldly philosophies, false doctrines, and even Church traditions can all play into a skewed perception of God. Or we may have a wrong perception of Him simply due to ignorance. We may readily see the Father as great, holy, exalted, and mighty, yet distant or indifferent to our personal needs. **Our theology may esteem Him as the omnipotent Heavenly Father of all, while our heart never enters the actual and real experience of trusting and knowing Him as our "*Dad*".**

A healthy relationship with an earthly father is one that grows and deepens through the years. A healthy relationship with God is one that grows and deepens with an ever unfolding revelation of who He is and who we are to Him. I can mark the seasons in my life by the different revelations of God I've received as He has worked in my life. Each fresh revelation brings breakthrough into a new place of intimacy and fellowship with Him. I came to Christ through the revelation of my need for Him as my *Savior*. True freedom came when I saw Him as my *Lord*. As I grew spiritually, He revealed Himself as the *Heavenly Lover of my soul*. I remember the season of the revelation of the Holy Spirit as He ushered me into a new relationship with Himself as my *Teacher* and *Helper*. Other seasons have brought deeper fellowship with God as my *Deliverer, Counselor, Potter, and Creator*. Then came the revelation of "*Abba Father*".

Jesus Called Him Abba Father

In the Old Testament, pictures of God's *fatherhood* were seen, but the term "Father" was never used when addressing Him. They felt that God Almighty was too holy to be addressed personally in such a familiar way. Nevertheless, the understanding was there and the knowledge of God included both paternal and maternal care. This was seen in the very names by which God revealed Himself such as: "*Jehovah-Jireh*" ("*The Lord will provide*"—Gen. 22:14), and "*El Shaddai*" ("Almighty; God who is the many breasted One"—Gen. 35:11; this name comes from the root word "*shadad*" meaning "to overcome" and is also connected to the Hebrew word "*shadayim*" which means breasts. This name is often linked to blessing and fruitfulness).

While God was referred to as a "Father" in the Old Testament, Jesus ushered in a whole new paradigm in which we not only see God as a Father, but know Him personally as our *Abba Father*. "Father" was Jesus' favorite term when praying or teaching about God and is recorded sixty-five times in the synoptic gospels (Matthew, Mark, and Luke), and over one hundred times in the book of John. Paul's New Testament letters also describe God as "Father" over forty times. The whole Old Testament had referenced Him as a Father only fifteen times.[1]

Jesus lived in daily fellowship with Abba Father. He was sent from the Father to remove everything that hinders us from knowing God as our Abba Father, too. Jesus taught that addressing God as *Father* was not merely *"a"* way to address Him, but as *"the"* way to approach and know Him (Mark 14:36). The apostle Paul also used this term (Rom. 8:15; Gal. 4:6).

Abba was an Aramaic term used by the Hebrews that was translated in other New Testament Scriptures by the Greek word "***Pater***." The English equivalent is "***Papa***" or "***Daddy***". The term *Abba* was used not only by little children in speaking to their fathers, but was used by older children and adults when addressing a father with whom they had a close relationship. It is a term that conveys both honor and reverence, yet with the warm sense of relationship.

Jesus is the Author – the progenitor – of those who know God as Abba (Papa). Even at twelve years of age, Jesus knew God was His Daddy and **He cultivated a heart that allowed *Abba Father* to father Him as His Son.** He lived in continual fellowship with Father's presence. This is the life we were created to know . . . one that is not only *born* of God, but is also *fathered* by God. The nature of fathering is centered in *relationship*.

> "And because you are sons, God has sent forth
> the Spirit of His Son into your hearts, crying Abba Father."
> Galatians 4:6

God is Spirit and not a man. The only way we can know God as Abba Father is by being born of His Spirit. Knowing God as *Abba (Papa)* may not only be radical compared to the Old Testament, it may be radical to you. You may even think calling Him "*Dad*" or "*Papa*" is not holy enough. But again, "*Papa*" and "*Dad*" are but the English equivalent to "*Abba*". The Aramaic term is no more "holy" than the English equivalent. Calling the Father *"Abba"* or *"Papa"* does not minimize holy reverence for Him. It simply expresses who He is to us. Calling God *"Abba"* or *"Papa"* is one of the highest ways of revering Him because it conveys an attitude, not of presumptuous familiarity, but of one who sees our life as His beloved child. It is a loving expression of a dependent child . . . after all, is that not how we are to enter the Kingdom?

Living in the reality of our Heavenly Father as our *"Papa,"* with every sense of holiness and righteous fear, is the understanding that the Son brought us. We must be a people who know how to tremble in His presence, and yet know His intimate fathering care. Too often, religion has taught us to be *"reverent,"* but not *intimate* with God. God wants to deliver us from every *empty* religious structure and immerse us into holy intimacy out of which we are spiritually birthed with divine authority. Jesus came with a new paradigm in which we *fear* God, not through religious ritual, but by a life born of His Spirit and given to honor Him with whole hearted love. Such a life trembles at His Word, *and* yet climbs into the arms of His embrace and cries, *"Daddy"*.

As for being "holy enough," holiness means to be *"set apart"*. The revelation of God's holiness causes us to see Him as *set apart* from all else and our life as being *set apart* for Him. The indwelling presence of the Holy Spirit given at new birth enables our spirit man to *see* God's holiness (John 3:3, 7).

Jesus said that to enter the kingdom of heaven we must be converted (changed) and become as little children (Matt. 18:3). The nature of a child is that they are simple; they believe what you tell them. They are trusting, forgiving, and are completely dependent. They also like work to be fun and creative! But foremost, a child looks to the parent as their source of help, guidance, protection, and provision. A child depends on a parent for direction.

This is how God wants us to relate to Him. Not as superficial, nor as distant. But as loving children to a **Holy Father** who dearly loves us and has a destiny and inheritance for us. As a good Father, He wants to *lift us up* into divine purpose and identity. He wants us to believe Him and depend on Him. He wants us to delight ourselves in Him. And foremost, He wants us to revere Him as greater than ourselves. After all, He is.

Spirit of Adoption

Self-centeredness separated mankind from the presence of God, but the blood of our Elder Brother brings us back to Father's arms where we become Father-centered. **Father sent Jesus not as *a* way, but as the *only* way to Himself.** No other name, religion, power or person has ever—nor can ever—open the realm of God's fathering presence to us but Jesus. He is the Door to Father's house and the Way to Abba's arms where we find life, identity, and purpose. There, God's presence satisfies our deepest need *and* longing. We were created for Him and for His presence in our inner man.

King Solomon, one of the greatest kings on earth, said he had looked everywhere in the world to find what *satisfies*. He experienced it all, but only found emptiness (Eccles.). The world can not satisfy the human heart and soul—only God can because He alone makes us complete.

The immensity of Father's love for us is seen in ***His*** own sacrifice of sending His Son to the cross. Too often, we readily see Jesus' sacrificial part, but not what the Father experienced. In my own role as a parent, I have learned that a true father or mother would rather give their own life than to see harm come to their child. Since Jesus and the Father are one, Abba Father was just as much involved in the crucifixion as Jesus was (John 10:30). He was there. He saw. He felt. He was *in* His Son working out our salvation.

The Father loves His Son, but He also loves those He created yet and are lost in an abysm of death. The only way to rescue them was to sow His Son into the earth as a seed that would bring forth a resurrection harvest of sons out of death and unto glory. Only through burial could the Holy Seed flourish into a vine with many branches that would fill the earth and release Father's kingdom.

Our Elder Brother's willing death paid the penalty of our sin and broke the yoke of a self-centered nature. He took our death and the curse that was upon us, and His resurrection restored life and connection to the Father. In Christ, we become a new creation with a new heart and spirit that looks to heaven and cries, *"Abba Father!"*

Father God established that eternal life is in His Son, *and he who has the Son has life. Anyone who does not have the Son of God, does not have life* (1 John 5:11-12). Those who have the Son have *abundant life* (Heb. 9:15; John 10:10). **Now look how wonderfully the Holy Trinity work together in this divine process called our** *salvation***:** Father awakens our heart to come to Jesus by sending the Holy Spirit to reveal truth to us and convict our heart regarding sin. As faith is conceived *and* repentance engaged, we reach out to receive the Son as our Lord and Savior. As we do, the life of the Holy Spirit is breathed into us and the miracle of new birth takes place . . . we are *born* of God. The Spirit of Christ delivers us from the kingdom of darkness and brings us into the kingdom of light. We are brought to Father as a new creation. *Old things are passed away and all things are become new* (2 Cor. 5:17).

We come to Father God with words of confession, humility, and repentance, yet the miracle of new birth is truly a divine mystery. We *engage the miracle* by coming to Jesus—renouncing sin, forsaking self, and embracing His Lordship. However, the new birth in Christ is an *act of the Holy Spirit* breathing new life into the lungs of our previously dead spirit man.

The Holy Spirit given to us is called the *Spirit of Adoption*. His indwelling presence makes us a legal heir of God with all accompanying rights and privileges. As God's child, we are no longer slaves to sin or orphans in the world. We are no longer fatherless (John 14:18). We do not have to "figure things out" for ourselves. We belong to God and to His family. We have continual access to Abba Father and to all His resources. **The Spirit of Adoption gives us a new framework for a new way of thinking and living, no longer for ourselves, but for God.**

Being fathered by God creates a new mindset for how we perceive and engage life.

A "Fatherless" Mindset	vs.	**A "Fathered" Mindset**
Sense of abandonment	*	Sense of belonging
Rejection issues	*	Grounded in love

Identity in things / others	*	Identity in God
Sees God as a taskmaster	*	Perceives God as loving
Fears failure	*	Expectation in God
Is law and works based	*	Works of faith
Seeks approval of man	*	Seeks the approval of God
Feels lonely	*	Fellowships with God / others
Tries to fill own needs	*	Looks to God for all things
Is suspicious of God / others	*	Trusts in God
Lives with worry / anxiety	*	Has peace and inner rest
Is performance driven	*	Is Presence led
Feels shame / condemnation	*	Is filled with glory
Is insecure	*	Is confident in God
Is jealous of others	*	Humbly prefers others
Accuses / blames others	*	Forgives
Seeks own prosperity	*	Seeks the good of others
Seeks own path	*	Seeks unity
Comfort in people / things	*	Finds comfort in God
Compares self with others	*	Delights in who they are
Lives in bondage	*	Lives in liberty
Loves conditionally	*	Loves unconditionally
Is self-guided	*	Is Father-counseled

Mindsets govern thought, direction, and choices, and thus destiny.

The *Spirit of Adoption* frees us from operating as one who is abandoned, lost, or alone. He grounds us in the Father's love that is in Christ, and fills the deepest recesses of our heart with the love of the Father (Rom. 5:5). In Christ, we no longer live in fear or bondage. We have open access to Abba Father at all times. **Being fathered by God awakens our inner man, restores our soul, and makes our mind sound.**

In the Old Testament Hebrew culture, adopted sons had the same rights, privileges, and standing as a birth-son. They were embraced just the same as a natural born son, and took on the father's name. In fact, I've been told that special laws were designed to protect them from abuse or abandonment. Galatians 4:7 says that we are sons of

God, and if sons, then also *heirs with Christ* (see also Rom. 8:17; Eph. 3:6; Titus 3:7).

Everything that the Father gave to Jesus, Jesus now shares with us, including the affairs of Father's kingdom (James 2:5). We are heirs of the same kingdom of power that Jesus demonstrated and proclaimed saying, *"Repent, for the kingdom of heaven is at hand"* (Matt. 4:17). We not only receive a new life in Christ, but a whole kingdom with a divine culture, government, and work that expresses the Father's life through His children.

Our Heavenly *Papa* wants us to know the truth about Him and His fathering care in our life. He is not distant; He is near. He is good, kind and compassionate. He is a loving and involved Father, and He is also One who is worthy to be revered with *highest honor*. **Father God wants to remove from within us every** *way* **or** *sense* **of separation from Him.**

Born of the Spirit

Being *born of God* is a supernatural act of God. We have been born of the flesh *by* flesh, but being born of the Spirit is *by* the Spirit (John 3:6). It happens when we believe on the Son (whom Father sent) and receive Him (John 1:12, 13). Receiving Jesus means we renounce the lordship of self and embrace His Lordship. We have been born of the flesh; now the Father calls us to return to Him and be born of His Spirit.

If we choose to exist apart from God now, we will exist apart from Him for eternity. But Romans 10:8-10 says that if we *confess* with our mouth that Jesus is Lord, and *believe* in our heart that God raised Him from the dead, then we will be saved. In God's Book, believing means action!

Salvation involves the *entire* surrender of the heart and life. Luke 6:45 says that from *out of the heart* the mouth speaks. When our heart is in agreement with the Spirit of God, our words carry the power of the Spirit for healing and deliverance. **God wants our heart and our words** (Isa. 29:13). Hosea 14:2 says, "Take words with you and return to the Lord." Words are important for God says that **He comes in response to our words** (Dan. 10:12) The Father wants our whole life, and both our heart and mouth are necessary to a life fully surrendered to Him. 1 John 1:9 says if we confess our sins, He is faithful and just to forgive our sins and cleanse us from all unrighteousness. The surrender of our heart and mouth to God isn't just at new birth, but is vital for our maturing as His sons and daughters as well.

God's will for every person is that we come to His Son and are made a new creation in Him (1 Tim. 2:4). Jesus takes us to the Father. Have you come to Jesus? If not, will you come now? If so, pray the following aloud:

Heavenly Father, You are the Father of all creation and are worthy to be honored. I confess that I have sinned and have lived my own way. I ask You to forgive me and wash me from all sin by the blood of Your Son, Jesus, who died on the cross to break the power of sin and death that has held me. I believe that You raised Jesus from the dead and He is now seated in heaven with You. I believe that through faith in Christ, I, too, can live in resurrection power of the Spirit. Jesus, I ask that You would come into my heart and be my Lord and Savior. I want to be a new creation. I give You my heart, soul, mind, and body. I give you all that I am and have. I forsake a life of sin and independence. I return to You, Father, and receive Your rightful place of counsel and guidance in my life. I give You my life to be an honor to You. I receive Your breath of life. I ask that You would fill me now with Your Holy Spirit. Baptize me with Your Spirit as is taught in Your Holy Word. Thank You, Father, for Your love and mercy. Thank You for a new identity in You and the divine destiny You have ordained for me. In Jesus' name, Amen.

Luke 15:10 says that the angels rejoice over each child of God born into the kingdom of heaven. Your birth causes heaven to sing for joy!

Personal Application:

1. What was your born-again experience like?
2. What are the different revelations God has given you of Himself?
3. Do you feel you have a "fathered" mindset or "fatherless" mindset?
4. How does it make you feel to call God "*Dad*" or "*Papa*"?

CHAPTER 5

Who *is* Your Daddy?

Some people never get to know their earthly fathers, Some know them well, others to one degree or another. Some fathers don't know how to be vulnerable, relational, or open. But Father God is very relational and wants us to intimately know Him. How do I know that? Because His Spirit moved on the hearts of more than forty men, over a period of 1600 years, to write, under His inspiration, the sixty-six books we know as the *Word of God*. God's loving heart toward us is declared on every page. These writers were fishermen, farmers, kings, prophets, judges, doctors, and shepherds—men of diverse backgrounds, yet inspired by one Holy Spirit. Father God did this so that we can know Him *and* who we are.

As Son of Man, Jesus lived on earth in the full purposes designed for Him from eternity. **His life and purpose was wrapped in His identity as Abba's Son. So is ours.** When we know our identity as Abba Father's sons and daughters, we know where we come from and where we are going. We know what we are to do. People long to know the answer to the questions of who am I, why do I exist, and where am I going? Life with Father gives us the answers. The very fact that Father bestows on us the incredible title of being "His children" demonstrates His heart toward us (1 John 3:1-3). He could have called us: subjects, slaves, servants, maids, purchased objects, owned items, etc. But He doesn't. He calls us His sons and daughters and He wants to shoot us like an arrow from His bow to hit the target of His divine purposes in the earth.

Let's look at what His Word says about Him.

1   He is the Father of Life

God is the Creator of life—the Author—of *all* created things, living and "non-living," seen and unseen. He framed the world by His Word so that what is seen came from what is not seen (Heb. 11:3). He created the heavens and stretched them out; He formed the earth and what comes out of it; He gives breath and spirit to the people who walk in it (Isa. 42:5). He is the source of all life (Acts 17:25). When we look at creation, we see the expression of God: His creativity, power, and His mysteries. We see the knowledge of Him through His creation. Thus, no person is without excuse regarding the knowledge of God (Rom. 1:20).

He is above all, through all, and in all (Eph. 4:6). Without Him nothing would exist that exists. There is one Father *from* whom all things come and we exist *for* Him (1 Cor. 8:6). He is the Everlasting Creator who never sleeps, but watches over His creation continually (Ps. 121:3).

When God created us, He called out our destiny before it was manifest—calling things that "were not" as though they were (Rom. 4:17). He created mankind in His own likeness; He is our Father and we are the work of His hands (Isa. 64:8). In Him we live, move, and have our being (Acts 17:28).

Father God not only creates life, but He resurrects to life what has been dead (Gal. 1:1; Rom. 6:4). He gave that same power to the Son (Jn. 5:21). We cannot give *eternal* life, but as God's sons and daughters we have been given the authority and power to raise the dead back to life by the Son who dwells in us (Matt. 10:8).

2   Father is a Husbandman

Father God is not only the Author of life, but He is the Husbandman, the divine Gardener of what He authors. As a husbandman, He is a *worker of the ground*. Look at what He brought forth from the ground—a son (Adam) for Himself! And *from* the son, He formed a daughter (Eve). Then He told man to work the ground, too. God's commission for us to cultivate the earth has never ceased, and it's more than just growing potatoes! He wants more sons and daughters. As the Father works in our garden, we, too, are to do His work in the place where He puts us.

Father tends carefully to His purposes in the earth. Some people ask, "If God watches over all things, then why does He allow so much suffering and pain in the world?" But God didn't cause the pain—we did. So what can we do? We can engage with Him to live as His care-takers of the earth to restore and rebuild, by the life of the Spirit, what sin has destroyed. The earth itself is longing for us to do this (Rom. 8:19).

Father God loves to work in gardens. He is seen many times throughout Scripture working in a garden:

- Man's commission from God began in a garden (Gen. 2:8).
- Man's bride was drawn from his side in a garden (Gen. 2:21-24).
- In the Old Testament, God refers to Himself as a *husbandman* and His son (Israel) as His *vineyard* (Isa. 5).
- In the Song of Solomon, the bride of Christ is described as a garden (Song of Sol. 4:15).
- Jesus embraced the *cup of suffering* in a garden (Mark 14:32-41).
- Jesus was buried and raised to life in a garden (John 19:38-42).
- Our heart is likened to a garden where God's Word is sown as seed (Mark 4:1-20).

Jesus referred to His Father as the *Heavenly Vinedresser* and Himself as the *True Vine*—versus Adam who had been an *"untrue"* son, and Israel a *"wild grape"* (John 15:1). **Jesus was a faithful Son and tender Vine that produced *good fruit* because He allowed Father to cultivate His life.**

As a husbandman, Abba Father cultivates our ground with a vision for a specific harvest. He is *committed* to our *land*, to the *seed* of His Word that He plants in us, and to the desired *harvest* He envisions for our life. In Scripture, *ground* can represent natural soil or the *soil of our heart*. *Seed* can represent *lineage* or *God's Word,* as well as representing the *message of His kingdom* (Mal. 2:15; Matt. 13:19; Luke 8:11). Satan tries to steal and destroy all good seed because these bring forth a harvest of inheritance for God.

Father's Care of His Garden

As a good husbandman, Father knows exactly what to do in each season of our life. After all, He is the one who established the seasons of His creation! So, too, He establishes and watches over our *appointed* times. **Our care is *never* outside the Father's watchful eyes as He works with infinite understanding and skill** (Isa. 40:28). He sends the rain of His presence to soak the soil of our heart, making it tender to receive His Word. The nutrient laden rays of the light that comes from His face toward us make us grow. Since the seed of His Word is incorruptible and remains forever, it is the soil of our *heart* that needs special care so that His Word can grow unhindered. God says we are to guard our heart for out of it spring the issues of life (Prov. 4:23). As we co-labor with Him in our garden, He will care for the seed of destiny within us. He says He is faithful to watch over His Word to bring it to full fruition (Jer. 1:12).

Like a good gardener, Father weeds out what doesn't belong in *His* garden. What He *doesn't* plant, He will pluck up by the roots (Jer. 31:28; Matt. 15:13). Weeds can spring up from seed dropped by birds, or seed that is carried by the wind. In Scripture, birds often represent demons. The seed they "drop" are troubling thoughts or temptation they want to grow in our garden. Wind often represents the storms of life that bring seeds from other places in the earth—seeds of doubt and fear. If allowed, they will root and multiply. Some weeds have root systems that crawl from one place to another. This is how worldly mindsets work as they subtly crawl into our thinking and take root. Colossians 2:8 says to *beware* of philosophies and man's traditions that are not of Christ that deceive and destroy us.

While the struggles we face in life seem to be mainly fought in the mind, it is the condition of the heart that determines agreement with the seed or weed that comes to take root. In fact, scientific study has discovered that our heart actually has a "brain" and that it monitors the validity and integrity of our thoughts. Thoughts are determined as "right" or "wrong" and then kept or thrown out according to the condition of our heart. It is with the heart that we choose between the tree of the knowledge of good and evil, or the tree of life. Choices spring from the heart. The heart and its thoughts need watching and cultivating because the heart is easily deceived (Jer. 17:9).

Father's work in our garden is constant. There are times He will make us rest so our soil will be ready to receive new seed for a new harvest. He will use circumstances to help "till" our heart, also making it ready to receive His Word. His presence in our garden works to break apart the hard places and remove stones of unbelief. He is ever working to make our heart a rich place for His Word to grow. He nourishes our heart with truth and love, but He also uses the "manure" of difficulties to increase fruitfulness. Father uses sharp instruments to trim us when we become "overgrown," and for pruning to cut away the last season's branches in order to make us *more fruitful*! Father labors in our life with *vision* for a *full* harvest, and in *ways* that will bring about greater fruitfulness for His glory (John 15:2).

In the garden of our inner man is where the likeness of the Son is formed. Jesus was called the Father's **"*tender plant*"** (Isa. 53:2). A *"tender plant"* is one that receives life and nutrient from another plant, as a baby to a mother. Jesus said, "Man shall not live by bread alone, but by every Word that proceeds from the mouth of God" (Matt. 4:4). We, too, are Father's "tender plants." We are absolutely dependent on His voice to give us life. **As we live by His Word and are nurtured by His Word (both written [*logos*] and spoken [*rhema*] Word), we will grow into strong *"oaks of righteousness"***

whose leaves are for the healing of the nations (Isa. 61:3). This is what Father desires in the garden that He plants.

3   He is the Father of Glory

Father God is the source of *glory*, that is, the presence of manifest worth, divine splendor, majestic wonder, and incomparable dignity. Scripture says that His glory is the wellspring of wisdom and revelation. His *glory* opens the eyes of our understanding to know Him, His eternal call on our life, and *His* inheritance in *us*! His glory is His manifest presence that causes us to *experience* the greatness of His power toward us (Eph. 1:17-19).

Father's glory raised Jesus from the dead; His glory brings us also into new life (Rom. 6:4). **Whenever you need resurrection life in some area, just ask for His glory!**

Jesus said we are not to seek the honor or glory that comes from people; we are to seek the glory and honor that comes from our Father (John 5:44; Rom. 2:7; John 8:50). In fact, as Jesus was about to go to the cross, He asked Father to glorify Him with the glory He had with God before the world existed (John 17:5). His first coming was as a humble baby; His second coming will be in the *glory* of His Father, accompanied by an angelic host (Mark 8:38).

Abba Father shares His glory with His Son, but not with another, and not with idols (Isa. 42:8; 48:10, 11). When we choose to be crucified with Christ and become one with Him, we are not *another*! As Jesus' body, we are given the great privilege of intimately knowing God's glory. To keep us from being defiled by agreement with what is "another," Father purifies our heart and motives—He wants us to be partakers of His glory. So the Heavenly Refiner's fire purges out *"mixture"* so we can experientially know His manifest worth and divine splendor (Mal. 3:3).

4   He is the Father of Lights

Father is the Source of all light, great and small. He is called the Father of the stars and the heavenly luminaries because He is their creator, upholder, and ruler. As the Source of light, He never changes—there is never a shadow, shade, or hint of darkness in Him, at all, ever. He is pure light and He has established various lights to govern the days and seasons of the earth. He appointed each one their place and their brilliancy. He put them into constellations by divine design so that the heavens declare His glory and the work of His hands (Ps. 19:1). The creation and salvation of mankind is the work of His hands! Psalm 19:2 says that the heavens pour forth their *speech* day to day, and night to night they display the knowledge of God.

As each star is in its appointed place, together their pattern tells the story of redemption. Astrology has twisted the meaning of God's design in the stars and have made a worship of them. But the truth is they speak of Jesus. The constellation Aires speaks of the sacrificial ram or Lamb slain for us; Lyra, the harp, speaks of praise; Coma (the woman and Child), speaks of the child who is the *Desire of the Nations*; Crux reveals the Cross; Andromeda (the chained woman) speaks of the captive daughter of Zion to be set free; and Leo declares the Lion of Judah. I could go on, but as you can see, Father set the stars in place to declare His glory and the wonder of His work with mankind.

Jesus, the Bright and Morning Star, said that we, too, are lights (Rev. 22:16; Matt. 5:14-16). The divine light within us illumines the way for others to know Jesus. And just as the stars, Father sets us into specific places. He appoints our place where He wants us to declare the work of His hands. This is why it is important to know the gifts and specific call He places on our life. If He has appointed us to be an apostle to the nations and we're sitting in an office, we will not shine in the scope and capacity designed for us by our Father. This is just as true if *we* want to be a pastor, but He has called us to business. We must let *Him* appoint our place.

As we are in our appointed place, Father will also connect us with divine relationships that *together* create a *multiplied* brilliance for the revealing of Christ in the earth. As we *shine together*, the unity releases exponential increase of the knowledge of Christ. My gift alone has a specific sphere of influence, but combined with others and their gifts, our light increases in brilliance and scope. Multiplication is an aspect of divine blessing and command. That's why it is important to stay in our appointed place and move only as

Father directs us. As His children, our life is about His glory being revealed in the earth.

Father's Government of Light

We spoke of the seasons of our life. Father governs our seasons with His light. **Even the "dark times" are never outside His government of light.** Micah 7:8 says, "When I sit in darkness, the Lord will be a light to me."

From Father's nature of light comes every good and perfect gift. His gifts carry the light of His goodness toward us—there is no hidden agenda with Him (James 1:17). If our heart is shadowed by dark thinking, we may see what He gives us as insufficient or not altogether good, but in truth, *all* He gives us is perfect and complete. Thankfulness removes any veil of sorrow so that our eyes see Him and His goodness that follows us *all* our days (1 Thess. 5:18; Ps. 23:6).

Just as earthly fathers love to give gifts to their children, Father loves to give us gifts (Matt. 7:11). Sometimes His gifts look just a little different than what we might expect! But His gifts are *always* good. And the good things He gives us, He doesn't take back. We may not receive it or engage it, but He doesn't take it back. If Father has given you something you haven't yet claimed, it's not too late—it is still waiting for you.

5   He is the Father of Mercies

Father is the source of mercy. Mercy is the nature of being compassionate, affectionate, loving, and tender toward the weak (2 Cor. 1:3). Father's nature of being merciful is a facet of His manifest glory (Exod. 34:6). He is the Fountain of compassion and His mercies are over *all* His works (Ps. 145:9). His compassion and mercy *cover* His works. **His mercies are new every morning and they remind Him continually of His covenants** (Ps. 106:45; Lam. 3:22, 23). Father's great mercy is the spring by which we are called His children. Because of His abundant mercies we live with *continual* hope and unceasing expectation (1 Pet. 1:3).

Our Father is *merciful* and gentle toward us because He knows our weakness and fragile make-up. He is mindful that we are made from mere dust (Ps. 103:13-14). He is patient with the stammering; compassionate with the sick; gentle with the ignorant; and merciful with the repentant child. Father loves all His children. He delights in our victories, but grieves at our waywardness. He so delights in us because of His great mercy that He calls us *"containers of mercy"* prepared for the riches of His glory (Rom. 9:23). His lovingkindness rests on us who fear Him, and He pours out His healing and deliverance on us so that His glory dwells in our land (Ps. 103:17; Ps. 85:9).

Jesus said we are to be merciful like our Father (Luke 6:36). God's Word says we are to *love* mercy—it is one of Abba Father's "lifestyle requirements" for all mankind (Mic. 6:8). He hears the cries of the hurting and needy continually. He wants *us* to hear their cries, too . . . and take action! We are His hands of mercy in the earth. Jesus said that as we show mercy to others, we, too, will receive mercy (Matt. 5:7).

6 He is a Father to the Fatherless and Judge of Widows

Father God is deeply moved by the helpless. His face looks to the poor, the fatherless, and the widow. Giving to the poor is so important to our Heavenly Dad that He says if we shut our eyes to their need, not only will our cry not be heard, but we will actually reap curses (Prov. 28:27; 21:13).

Regarding the fatherless, He says that when earthly parents fail or forsake us, He will take us up in His arms (Ps. 27:10). His eyes are attentive to those who have no father and He is adamant about our care for them. As He cares for us, we are to care for them; He commands us to father them—**this is the heart of *true* religion** (Ps. 68:5; James 1:27).

Psalm 68:5 also describes our Father as a judge of the widows. This means He stands on their behalf with justice. Generally speaking, widows are frail, vulnerable, dependent, and often without needed help and proper support. We hear reports all the time about those who prey on the elderly, seeking to take advantage of their vulnerability. Because Father cares for them, He rises up to defend them. He defends them through us and our care for them. As His children we are commanded to put on His compassion and take care of the widows.

Our Father is a good Father who watches over the earth and over our lives. We have read in this chapter of who He is as the source of life, glory, lights, and mercy, as well as a Father to orphans and widows. These are just a few aspects of how He describes Himself in His Word. The more we learn of Him, the more we see there is to know. The knowledge of God is ever unfolding!

Personal Application:

1. In what ways does Father want you to "cultivate the earth"?
2. In what ways do you see Father cultivating your life?
3. In what ways have you seen or experienced His glory?
4. Do you know your "appointed place"?
5. How have you experienced Papa's mercies? How have you been merciful?
6. In what ways do you help the poor, fatherless, and widows?

CHAPTER 6

The Father and His Sons

I n this chapter we are going to continue looking at who our Father is, but more specifically with *whom* He interacts as a Father. Let's see what Scripture says about these relationships.

1   Abba Father and the Son

> "So that with one accord you may with one voice
> glorify the God and Father of our Lord Jesus Christ."
> Romans 15:6

The more we see how Jesus was fathered by Abba Father, the greater understanding we have of Abba's fathering in our own life. As we learned in Chapter One, Jesus lived from the "God-grid" as the source of His perspective and supply for all His needs. His expectations and perspectives were centered in His Father, not man. I think a lot of the pain we experience in life is because our expectations are centered in people and circumstances. And when loss and disappointment happen, where do we go? What do we do? Father wants to be our source of expectation and perspective.

Jesus knew His identity—where He came from, where He was going, and what He was to do. He understood who He was as a Son, and thus declared that Father was *greater than Himself* and honored Him as such (John 14:28; 16:28). He knew His identity because of Abba's fathering presence in His life. Jesus knew His identity in *connection with Abba Father and the Holy Spirit.* And in that connection, He lived in a realm of feeling *safe*. He was not alone. He was loved. He was cared for.

Were dynamics perfect at home with His earthly family? I highly doubt it! He had human parents and unregenerate siblings. What more do I need to say? Painful words and unloving actions could have established lies in Jesus' mind about God, others, or Himself. But He was born of the Spirit, walked as truth incarnate, and was rooted in Abba's love, thus there was no place *in* Him for lies to take root or wounds to fester. Father God wants us to live in these same dynamics of intimate connection with the Holy Trinity. He wants us rooted in Him and His love.

Father and Son are One

As Son of Man, it *delighted* the Father to fill Jesus with the *fullness* of God—filling the Son with the presence of the Father and power of the Spirit (Col. 1:19, 20). It delighted the Father that Jesus' work on the cross would reconcile all things back to Himself. Father sent His Son to be the Savior of all mankind who were created in His own image, the image of the Godhead (1 John 4:14; John 3:16). The Son didn't come on His own behalf or impulse, but He came from Father; *They are One* (John 8:42). **The very works Jesus did were the manifestation of the Father working through Him.** That's why Jesus said, "If you've seen Me, you've seen the Father" (John 14:9-10).

The relationship between the Father and Son is the wellspring of understanding for who we are as Father's children. Our life as the body of Christ is not about rites and traditions, but about relationship with the Father, Son, and Holy Spirit. It is Father's *good pleasure* that we, like Jesus, are filled with the fullness of God, ministering His life to the world around us.

All religions, *except Christianity*, minister from an expectation of performance, rituals, and rites. Jesus ministered out of *relationship*. Scripture says that no one has ever seen God except the only Begotten One who is in the very *bosom* (heart) of Father. From *that* intimate place, Jesus reveals the Father to us (John 1:18). Without the Son we cannot know the Father for the revelation of the Father is *hidden* in the Son. And the revelation of the Son is unfolded by the Spirit. **As Jesus' body, we are brought into the *bosom (heart)* of the Father to know Him and see Him, and then to declare Him to the world.**

Jesus declared that the Father is a *living Father*, and that He lives because of the Father. We, too, live by *feeding* on the living Son (John 6:57). The Heavenly Father is not a distant "Force" or a dead god. Dead gods produce dead worshippers. If we are dead, then we are feeding on what is dead. The Living God produces living sons and daughters whose lives *flourish* because of intimate fellowship with Him and His living Son. We don't live and flourish because we follow a religion, but because we *eat* the Word of life that comes from the Father (Matt. 4:4).

Jesus emphasized that His words were not His own, but the Father's. As He listened to His Father, He spoke what He heard Him say. Jesus didn't talk about Himself, but about the Father, what He heard *from* the Father, and what the Father showed Him (John 12:49, 50; John 8:26, 28). Jesus did ***nothing independent*** of the Father or the Spirit of His Father. This is our model as Father's children.

Abba Father Supported His Son

The *spirit of the world* hates Jesus because Jesus doesn't coddle sin, but calls sin and evil for what they truly are—wickedness against Father God (John 7:7). In John 15:23, Jesus said whoever hates Him, hates the Father. **We live in a world that is at *enmity* with the Father, Son, and Holy Spirit** (James 4:4). This is evident in our own culture of how current *interpretation* of laws now separate church and state, have replaced the teaching of God in public education for teaching of humanism, and instated censorship of Christian faith in the work place. Media bias and other cultural influences seek to silence the voice of God and the mention of Jesus' name. These are not mere happenstances, but are the spirit of the world and the spirit of antichrist at work. The spirit of antichrist hates the Father.

The Son of God walked on earth *openly declaring* His love for the Father, and the Father openly declared His love for His Son (John 17:25, 26). Father didn't send His Son alone, but with the testimony that He Himself had sent Him (John 5:37; 8:18). He "backed up" His Son. The testimony of the Holy Spirit backed Him up, too. **So much so, that God's Word says the one who doesn't believe on Jesus as the Son of God is calling all *Three* a liar!** (1 John 5:6-12)

As sons and daughters of God, we, too, are given the confidence that we are *backed* by God as we seek His heart and do His will. He says that His eyes look continually throughout the whole earth to show Himself strong on behalf of those whose heart is completely His (2 Chron. 16:9). He does not send us into the world with a divine commission and then leave us on our own. That is not His nature.

Abba Father was well pleased with His Son and backed Him with the power of testimony. The ***Law of Moses*** testified of Him as well as the ***prophets*** (Acts 28:23). The ***Father's own voice*** testified saying *"This is My beloved Son with whom I am well-pleased,"* and the ***Holy Spirit's power and presence*** testified of Him as being the Son of God (John 3:16, 17). Jesus didn't testify about Himself, but He told people that if they didn't believe He was *in* the Father and the Father *in* Him, to at least believe Him for the very ***works*** that He did because His works glorified the Father (John 5:31; 10:25; 14:11). God's Spirit *in* us and work *through* us also testifies that *we* are His sons and daughters.

Jesus was never alone; Father was always with Him because Jesus always did the things that pleased Him (John 8:29). Even in Jesus' darkest moment, while taking our sins upon Himself, He may have *felt* abandoned by God, but Father was right there with Him (John 16:32). Abba was there even when others ran away. Maybe you are going through a time like that, too, as others have seemingly abandoned you. You may feel that God has abandoned you, too. But Father is there. Even in the midst of fiery trials, He does not forget His child. He does not forsake you.

Father God did not forsake His Son; Jesus went humbly to the cross in absolute submission to Father's will. Father says that He *looks to* the humble (Isa. 66:2). If Father had forsaken His Son, how could Jesus have committed His spirit into Father's hands? (Luke 23:46). So why did Jesus cry out, *"My God, My God, why have You forsaken Me?"* Because He also experienced the Father's judgment and wrath that was upon the sin He bore for us. Sin turns away the face of God (Isa. 64:7).

Jesus experienced *our* state of separation from God. He brought that *state* to the judgment seat of God on the cross so that we no longer have to live in that condition. God says we are to remember His goodness *and* the pit from which we have been taken (Isa. 51:1). Remembering makes us continually thankful for what we've been given. Some people may forget what their old life without God's presence was like, but I can never forget the abyss of darkness of what it feels to have God's face turned away because of sin. I never want to return to that place again. Father hates sin and He turns His face away from iniquity, but He looks to the humble and He does not forsake His obedient child.

The Son had Freewill

Abba Father *loved* Jesus and the fact that He willingly laid down His life as a good Shepherd for the life of the sheep. Jesus did this so that we could fellowship with the Father, just as the Father and Jesus fellowship together (John 10:11-18). No one took the Son's life from Him. He willingly laid it down on His own initiative, yet with the understanding that He had the power and authority to pick His life back up again should He choose to do so. Father gave Him that authority and power, but He didn't pick His life back up, *He let Father raise Him.* Our Father gives us the same authority and power to lay our life down or pick it up. But here is where we often have difficulty; we lay our life down, and then we pick it up ourselves! There *is* a rising up through the power of the Spirit in us that is different from raising ourselves up by carnal mindsets and means. That's why the apostle Paul said, "I die *daily!*" (1 Cor. 15:31). When *Father* raises us up, it is by the Spirit of holiness with *power*; the way of the flesh makes us *powerless* in the spirit realm. The mind of the Spirit knows the difference—that's why continual communion with the Father, Son, and Holy Spirit teach us to know the difference as we wait on Him.

Jesus had freewill. So do we. Some people think that in yielding their lives to God they are really saying, "I give You *control*." God doesn't want to *control* us. Controlling another person is manipulation rooted in self-centeredness and fear. That is not Father's nature! **He doesn't want to *control* us—He doesn't want robots.** Jesus was not a robot. Jesus did what He did out of love, not control. Jesus was led by the Spirit because He was willing to follow the Spirit. **Love follows God's leadership and moves with Him.** It's like dancing with God!

This aspect of the Son's choice to lay down His life, knowing He had the right and power to take it up again is a central part of our own walk with Father. The foundation of our walk of salvation is a life laid down. As we do—and *only* as we do—can we then experience the power of being raised up with resurrection life. As sons and daughters of God, the cross was not just what Jesus did *for* us, but is the model He gave *to* us as a life laid down for the love of the Father and doing His will. And what we surrender will be returned "*a thousand times over*" in myriad ways.

Listen to the words of C. G. Trumbull who wrote the following:

"Genesis 22:16-18 says, '...Because you have done this thing, and have not withheld your son, your only son, I will bless you, and I will greatly multiply your seed as the stars of the heavens and as the sand which is on the seashore; and your seed shall possess the gate of their enemies. In your seed all the nations of the earth shall be blessed because you have obeyed My voice.' And from that day to this, men have been learning that when, at God's voice, they surrender up to Him the one thing above all else that was dearest to their very hearts, that same thing is returned to them by Him a thousand times over. Abraham gives up his one and only son, at God's call, and with this disappears all his hopes for the boy's life and manhood, and for a noble family bearing his name. But the boy is restored, the family becomes as the stars and sands in number, and out of it, in the fullness of time, appears Jesus Christ."

"This is just the way God meets every real sacrifice of every child of His. We surrender all and accept poverty; and He sends wealth. We renounce a rich field of service; He sends us a richer one than we had dared to dream of. We give up all our cherished hopes, and die to self; He sends us the life more abundant, and tingling joy. And the crown of it all is our Jesus Christ. We can never know the fullness of the life that is in Christ until we have made Abraham's supreme sacrifice. The earthly founder of the family of Christ must commence by losing himself and his only son, just as the Heavenly Founder of that family did. We cannot be members of that family with the full privileges and joys of membership upon any other basis." [1]

The Son Carried the Father's Heart

Because Father and Jesus are one, Jesus, too, carries a fathering heart. He is even called the "Everlasting Father" (Isa. 9:6). As we say, "Like Father, like Son". As a good Shepherd, He fathers the sheep that Father has given to Him. The Father has given us into Jesus' hands to keep us safe, just as an earthly father would do in handing the care of younger children to a trusted elder son. We are His sheep and we follow Him. He knows us and no one will ever be able to snatch us from His hands, nor from the hands of our Father who is greater than all (John 10:27-29).

Eternal life is in the Son and He is our place of safety; He keeps us safe in Father's *name* (John 17:12). "Safe" doesn't always necessarily mean the absence of trial and painful circumstances. The key here is being *kept in His name*; name means nature. Our help is in His name (Ps. 124:8). Daniel 11:32 says that those who know their God (knowing His name and nature) *"shall be strong and do exploits"*. In the back of this book you will find a list of some of the names of God. May you be filled with the intimate knowledge of His name as you study them!

Father and Son Honored One Another

Abba Father loves the Son and has given *all* things into His hands for custody, care, keeping, and judgment (John 3:35). "All things" includes the intimate knowledge of the Father. Matthew 11:27 says that no one knows the Son, except the Father, and no one knows the Father except the Son, and to whoever the Son chooses to reveal Him. Jesus embraces full responsibility for what has been given Him. Even when on earth, He embraced *accountability* for all Father gave Him to do as having come from Abba Father and going back to Him (John 13:3).

Accountability is an expression of honor for one we esteem as *greater than ourselves*. Jesus honored the Father through accountability for what had been given Him. God says, "...for those who honor Me I will honor, and those who despise Me will be lightly esteemed" (1 Sam. 2:30). Personally, I feel accountable with the life given to me. I would not be here but for the divine intervention of God in my life and I am continually aware that my breath comes from Him. Some people don't feel accountable to God for the life, talents, or call given them—even some Christians. But we *are* accountable to God, and when you walk in it, it is both a reverential fear and a *delight*. Accountability is about honor and relationship with the Father, Son, and Holy Spirit. As God's children, we have been given everything we need for life and godliness for the doing of Father's will; we are accountable for what we've been given. Jesus said, "To whom much is given, much shall be required" (Luke 12:48).

Two things that hinder a life from esteeming Father as being greater than ourselves are *ignorance* and *pride*. Ignorance may stem from not having heard truth, while pride (tragically) states, "*I* am greater than all!" Father *requires* us to *walk humbly* with Him (Mic. 6:8). Yes, the Father has requirements of His children! He says we are not to be ignorant, but are to *study* to show ourselves proven workmen without shame (2 Tim. 2:15). Ignorance leads to ruin and pride to destruction (Hos. 4:6; Prov. 16:18).

Jesus' life was *set apart* for the Father to bring Him glory (John 10:36; 12:28). All God's children are a people *set apart* as "glory vessels". **Jesus didn't come seeking His own glory. He didn't need to—Father sought glory for Him, and therefore, also judgment** (John 8:49, 50, 54). Jesus said that His own glory was simply that of Father Himself—a glory that He knew before the world was created (John 17:5). As for judgment, Jesus didn't come to judge, but to save. Nevertheless, His judgments would have been correct because His perspectives were purely the Father's perspectives

(John 8:16). How many "judgments" do we make that are purely God's perspectives?

Although Jesus didn't come to judge, there *is* a judgment by the Son that is coming, for Father has committed judgment to the Son. That's why all mankind are to honor the Son whom the Father sent. We *cannot* honor Father unless we are honoring His Son. The one who doesn't honor the Son, doesn't honor the Father who sent Him (John 5:22, 23). Dishonor reaps judgment.

Jesus glorified Father by doing and *finishing* the work given Him to do (John 16:10; 17:4). His work was finished when He returned to the Father. Because Jesus finished His work, Father exalted and honored Him. Father wants us to finish the work He gives us to do and not stop halfway through. It's one thing to start a work and another to *finish* it! **The greatest honor we give to any father is obeying and fulfilling the tasks they assign us, whether at home, work, church life, etc.** When my children were young, their obedience was a sign of honor. We honor Father God by completing our assignment that He gives us, and He in turn will honor us with eternal rewards.

The Son's Unconditional Surrender

According to Father God, obedience is a demonstration of our love for Him. Jesus said, "But so that the world may know that I love the Father, I do *exactly* as the Father commanded Me..." (John 14:31). He didn't put conditions on what He would or wouldn't do. He lived surrendered to the Father's will, always following the leading of the Spirit (Acts 1:2). Jesus embraced Father's will even when it was a *cup of suffering* (John 14:31; 18:11). Why did Abba give Him the cup of *suffering*? As a parent, I'd do anything to keep my children from suffering, especially death. But one time, not long ago, Father taught me about the greatness of His love that would put such a cup in His own Son's hands. At the time, our son was at a point in his own journey with God called the *valley of decision*. He, like all of us, had made many good choices, as well as mistakes. But now he had come to a crucial crossroads—a critical moment that would determine his future. I stood before him and for the first time, as a parent, I was overwhelmed with the thought that if I could have given my life for him so that he would choose God's way, I would have done it, right then and there without hesitation. Thanks to God's love and grace, my son did make the right choice and he is now on the path Father designed for Him.

But in that brief moment, I caught a glimpse of just how much the Father loves us. Father, as a loving parent, was willing to give over to death the One He counted most precious in order to redeem wayward man back from death. Our Heavenly Father didn't throw us away when we fell in darkness. He didn't say, "Oh, well." Instead, He paid for our return to life with the blood of His own Son. And He didn't just send His Son to die for us. Father was *in* Jesus, experiencing death right there with Him on the cross. He did it for us. No one can tell me that if the Father and Son are one, that Papa didn't experience what Jesus was going through. He was not an indifferent onlooker.

And what's more, the Father got His Son back, yet not alone, but with many more sons and daughters. **Father made that** *cup of suffering*—**drunk by one**—**to become the** *cup of blessing* **to be drunk by all, thereby bringing many sons and daughters to glory** (Heb. 2:10; 1 Cor. 10:16). Jesus willingly drank the cup of suffering to give "*Himself for our sins, so that He might rescue us from this present evil age, according to the will of our God and Father*" (Gal. 1:4). In this, Father was, is, and will be glorified. Because of Jesus' willing sacrifice, Father raised Him from the dead and the Son is now seated with Father in heaven (Acts 2:32-33).

If you are drinking a cup of suffering right now, continue committing yourself and the situation to your Father. Don't stop putting your trust in Him who loves you and is able to make it become a cup of blessing. You may be suffering in some issue with health, finances, or relationship, but your Father is able to do abundantly above and beyond what you could ask or think (Eph. 3:20). His path of life sometimes takes us through the valley of the shadow of death, but victory always awaits us. Keep your eyes on Him. Trust Him, His timing, and His way.

> "*When I cannot understand my Father's leading,*
> *And it seems to be but hard and cruel fate,*
> *Still I hear that gentle whisper ever pleading,*
> *God is working, God is faithful, ONLY WAIT.*" [2]

2   The Father and Believers

There is no greater gift that we could ever receive than that of being called—by God Himself—His son or daughter. If you have been born of God's Spirit, then God is your Father and you are His child (2 Cor. 6:18). This means we get to be *childlike*! Everyone comes into Father's kingdom as a child—trusting, unpretentious, and dependent . . . and happy! Father knows those who are His; we are not forgotten or unnoticed. We don't have to worry about being left in the car, lost in the crowd, or abandoned on a street corner. All our needs are in His care.

Loving Obedience Draws the Manifest Presence of the Father

Father is our source for all things; as His children we exist *for* Him (1 Cor. 8:6). Jesus said the Father loves those who love His Son, and that our love for the Son is shown by acting on His words (John 14:15; 16:27). We are known as Father's children because we do His will, just as Jesus did (Matt. 12:50). We are **chosen by the Father** and **sanctified by the Holy Spirit** to **obey the Son** (1 Pet. 1:2). Sanctified means to be separated from what is common, purified for divine use, and dedicated to God.

Loving obedience draws the presence of God to our life. It's like a spiritual magnet. Obedience draws the intimate presence of Christ (John 14:20-23). Jesus likes His sheep to follow Him! It is no different with a parent toward a child; when a child is obedient, there is sweet fellowship. Faith, love and obedience create an ambient to which Jesus and the Father delight to come and make their presence known. What does the manifestation of their presence look like? We experience God's presence as peace, wisdom, revelation and His voice of counsel. We experience strength and hope, and we may even feel physical effects of His power and nearness. We feel deep reverence and a connection to Him and His world. These are just for starters.

But what about an obedient life that looks to Father for some needed help, but help seems to be delayed? What releases the manifestation of provision in our life? All things come through faith. If it tarries, listen, believe, do what He says, and *expect* Him to move on your behalf. Hopelessness and hope deferred are the voice of the enemy. Father works to fulfill much more than what we know—in us, in those around us, and for the purposes He has for us in the days ahead. He may need to do something *in* us, first. We do not always know the reason of delay, but He does, and He will guide our steps as we look to Him, and will work to bring about His full purposes in us.

Spiritual warfare may also be an issue that is hindering us. As we spend time in God's presence, He will show us what we are to do and even *how* we are to pray. Remember, Father is a military leader, judge, and disciplinarian. His plan with our life is vast and far-reaching, more than we know. Difficult times, when we feel isolated by some circumstance, are often times when God works most. Our prayers are not unheard and our need is not out of His sight.

As Abba Father's children, we are *in* Him because we are in Jesus, and Jesus is in us, and Jesus is in the Father. That statement makes me dizzy, but it shows the oneness we have with both the Father and Son. The divine Life *within* us is a mystery, a gloriously divine mystery! (Col. 2:2). It can't even be comprehended by the natural mind because it is a supernatural act of God that happens by *His* will, not by the will of the flesh or man (John 1:13). When we draw near to Him through the way He has given us, He draws near to us (James 4:8). This is His promise.

Family Life with Brothers and Sisters

Being born of God makes us brothers and sisters with *all* who are born of the Spirit. We have Father's name (and nature) and are kept in His name (John 17:11). We, together, are **one in Christ.** Our unity together glorifies Father and draws His blessing (Rom. 15:6; Ps. 133). This unity *is* possible because we have the same indwelling Spirit (1 Cor. 12:13-14). Together we make up the body of Christ. We are not one member, but many; ***each one of us*** is a special part of the body that adds a specific dynamic that holds the body together. This makes us to function effectively as Jesus' body for Father's work in the earth (Eph. 4:16).

Father says we are to treat one another with love, respect, and honor (Mal. 2:10). As brothers and sisters, life together is not always perfect. That means attitudes can be skewed, actions may sometimes be unloving, and words may occasionally be curt. We may feel overlooked or even rejected. But we are a family, and specifically—God's family! We are commanded by Father to love one another, prefer one another, forgive one another, and esteem one another. If there is dissention, discord, or division, we must check our own heart first to see what area of sin, self, or pride may be operating . . . and get rid of it! Father hates division and strife (Prov. 6:16-19). If we say we love Him, but do not love our brother, we are walking in darkness and do not know Him (1 John). We can have all the spiritual gifts and wonderful talents and abilities to minister, but if we do not love, we are just clanging cymbals that make a lot of noise (1 Cor. 13:1). We are not Father's only child and we need one another.

Our Wonderful Elder Brother

Jesus is the Firstborn among many brothers and sisters and He is not ashamed to be called our Brother (Rom. 8:29; Heb. 2:11). He willingly delighted in becoming like us in order to redeem us (Heb. 2:17). He not only treats us as treasured brothers and sisters, but as His intimate friends—not as slaves, or younger siblings with whom He can't relate, or who are a nuisance to Him. He explained that friends share hearts and plans, something you don't do with a servant (John 15:15). In the Old Covenant, God's people understood duty. In Christ, we understand duty with divine purpose and intimacy. Jesus is our Friend who shares the Father's heart and eternal plans with us. When we join ourselves to Jesus, we become one Spirit with Him (1 Cor. 6:17).

As God's children we have an enemy—God's enemy—the devil. Scripture says that the devil stands before Father in heaven accusing us day and night, but our Elder Brother, Jesus, is our Advocate (Rev. 12:10). As Father looks on Jesus' pierced hands, feet, and side, Satan's words are thrown out of court. We need to throw them out, too! If the devil's words have no standing before Father, why should we embrace them in our own thinking? Satan likes to make us think we have to "pay for our own sin" through *self-beating* like false religions do, but the blood of Christ is sufficient for our cleansing. **In Christ, there is no condemnation to those who *do not* walk after the flesh, but *after* the Spirit** (Rom. 8:1). Jesus' blood has washed away *all* our sins. We are without guilt *and* shame as long as we do not insult the Spirit of grace by continuing in sin.

Father's nature hates sin and loves righteousness. His nature in us makes us not want to sin! However, if we stumble, His throne of grace and mercy is *always* open 24 / 7. Satan likes to keep us in condemnation if we stumble or fall. He likes to accuse us even when we haven't done anything wrong! He likes to keep us in condemnation or shame, **but the *life of the Spirit* is one of continual cleansing truth and joyful embrace in Father's arms.**

One day we will be with Jesus and we will see Him in the full glory that Father has given Him—the glory given Him before the foundation of the world. And yet, Jesus also said that He has given us the same glory that the Father gave to Him. **God's glory makes us one just as the Father and Son are one** (John 17:22-24). He says that one day His glory will *cover* the earth (Hab. 2:14). That glory will be manifest through the unity of love among the sons and daughters of God.

Children of Truth

As God's children, we are sons and daughters of truth. We have been rescued from deception and death by embracing the love of the truth (2 Thess. 2:10). Instead of buying into the lies of the devil as we did when we were ignorant, we now learn to ***know truth*** and ***apply truth*** in all of life. Our relationship with God is not about a focus on "law," but about ***obedience to truth*** (1 Pet.1:22). Upholding the laws of God is a fruit of obeying the One who *is* truth. Eternal life is in *knowing* the Father and the Son, not in how well we do at "being good". A person can be excellent in appearance and never know God. John 17:3 says, *"This is eternal life, that they may know You, the only true God, and Jesus Christ whom You have sent."* Adherence to truth is practiced by letting God write His law of love on our heart. Sometimes that "writing" is painful! But we can only truly know Him as we learn to fully love and obey Him. Intimacy with truth results in a transformed life.

Father's work in our life is accomplished through the joint work of the Spirit and the Son. Father draws us to Jesus and gives our care into His hands; the Son promises to *never turn us away* (John

6:65). Jesus said that all who the Father had given Him would come to Him, but also that no one could come to Him unless the Father draws him (John 6:37; 6:44). We learned earlier that whatever Jesus hears from Abba Father, He tells us about it; we don't ever have to live in the dark regarding our Father's will and purposes (John 14:7-9). Through Jesus, we are given the Spirit without measure; the Spirit gives us the same access to Father that Jesus has (John 3:34; Eph. 2:18).

Affirmed as His Children

Father God acknowledges us and affirms us as His children. We may feel unrecognized by man for who we are, or things we've done. Our service may seem hidden while others receive accolades. But just as the Father affirmed Jesus, He affirms us. In the realms of God's kingdom you and I are known and affirmed as an esteemed son and daughter of God. In fact, *we are the display of His manifold wisdom before principalities and powers in the heavens* (Eph. 3:10). One day, we will experience our own name honored in heaven as Jesus stands before Father and His angels and declares our name (Rev. 3:5). Imagine that!

A Family of One Spirit

As God's children we have not been given the *spirit of the world*, but the *Spirit of God* so that we can freely know the things God has given us (1 Cor. 2:12). When Jesus returned to heaven, the next step in God's perfect plan was to send the Holy Spirit for the empowering of His children. As Father had given Jesus custody of all things regarding us, that now included the sending of the promise of the Holy Spirit. There are two significant *impartations* we experience with the Holy Spirit that enable us to be daily *filled* and *led* by the Spirit. They are:

- Being born of the Spirit (John 3:5-7)
- Baptism of the Holy Spirit and fire (Matt. 3:11; Acts 1:8; 2:4)

Jesus Himself as Son of Man was born of the Spirit, full of the Spirit, baptized of the Spirit, and led of the Spirit. In fact, the Holy Spirit not only led Jesus *prior* to His death, He continued to lead Him *even after His resurrection from the dead*! (Acts 1:2) The Spirit and the Son do everything together. As sons and daughters, we must do everything with the Spirit, too!

As God's children, we are given the Holy Spirit as our Helper, Teacher, and Comforter to be with us *forever* (Acts 2:33). Jesus walked in continual fellowship with the Holy Spirit and submitted Himself to the Spirit's leading. As God's children, we will never cease to need the constant presence, power, and guidance of the Holy Spirit. Though the Holy Spirit is not seen with the natural eye, His presence, comfort, and power is real, felt, and effective in and through our life. The Spirit guides us in all truth, reveals Jesus to us, and imparts to us all that belongs to our Elder Brother and the One who is our Head.

The Holy Spirit teaches us the mysteries of God and what has been hidden for us. He searches the depths and thoughts of God to reveal them to us (1 Cor. 2:9-11). He testifies about the Son to us and reminds us of the Son's words (John 14:26; 15:26-27). He speaks words of encouragement, wisdom, counsel, revelation, and knowledge. His voice may be as thoughts, impressions, pictures, words, feelings, or even a physical sensation. He reminds us of truth as we minister to others. He doesn't speak about Himself, but speaks what He hears from Father. He reveals to us what is to come. The Spirit's presence in us and upon us moves us to speak to others of Jesus. That's what He loves to do most! (John 16:12-13)

Father wants us to tell others about Jesus. Jesus Himself has commanded us to go and teach all nations what He has taught us (Matt. 28:19). Remember, the blessing of divine life given to us is meant to flow out of us as rivers of living water so that *all* men come to the knowledge of the truth and are saved. This is Father's will (1 Tim. 2:4).

As sons and daughters of God, we are going to shine like the sun forever in our Father's kingdom (Matt. 13:43). That is what Jesus said! That light in us is Christ Himself who is the Light of the world. His presence in us makes *us* light in this world—a world of men, women, and children whom Father loves, but are lost in darkness. May we give our life to shine with His light to them (Matt. 5:14).

3   Father and His Son, Israel

This topic is a book in itself—even volumes! However, I'll be brief. Read the whole Bible. In it you will find that God's covenant relationship with Israel has never ended. As Israel's Father, everything that concerns that people is a matter of concern to Him who is the God of Israel (Jer. 31:9). **Father's covenant with Israel has never ended; it just changed leadership from the house of Moses to the house of Jesus** (Jer. 31:31-33; Heb. 8:8-13). In fact, the New Covenant we have been given from the Father was first given to Israel—we are just privileged to be grafted in (Rom. 11:1-5). Just because the Jews rejected the Mediator of the New Covenant does not negate the truth that it was given to them. Remember, Father doesn't take back His gifts. The New Covenant is still theirs. However, as with any gift, we have the choice to receive it or not. Someday their eyes will be open to what's been given them and they will receive Him. They will open the gift of Father's New Covenant in Christ and see the One who they pierced (Rev. 1:7). In fact, many have and many more are receiving Him even now.

Father Himself also gave Israel the land where they are now occupying (Gen. 13:15, 17; 15:18; Josh. 21:43). It belongs to Israel no matter who else tries to claim it. Israel belongs to God and His eyes are continually on that *land* as *His* own (Deut. 11:12; 33:13). No wonder there is so much war over that small area of soil—it is a spiritual warfare between the will of God and Satan's desire for what belongs to God.

Father's faithfulness to Israel stands as an ensign of His faithfulness to us. God does not forsake His children. He still loves Israel, and as a true Father He will never throw His son away (read Hosea). He will work to perfect what He has begun in His sons and daughters until Jesus' return (Phil. 1:6). What a promise!

Personal Application:

1. When was the last time you heard Father's voice affirming you?
2. Do you feel accountable for the life and call Father has given you?
3. In what ways do you express an attitude that Father is greater than you?
4. Do you find unity with other Christians easy or difficult? Why?
5. How do you feel about Israel as God's son?

CHAPTER 7

Dad is There for You

Father God wants us to see Him as being involved in every detail of our life. 1 Peter 5:7 says that God cares *for* us. Many times we automatically interpret that to mean He cares *about* us, but it means what it says—He cares *for* us. He has "charge" of our well-being.

Each one of us has gone through times when we've thought, *"Where are You, God? Do you really care what I'm going through? Do You see? Do You have a plan for my life?"* We want to experience the reality of our theology regarding His care. We want to know Him in our circumstance and experience His involvement and not feel that He is simply watching from afar. One time I was rehearsing the *"why"* question to God about a loss I was going through, questioning His care, when I heard Him say, *"How can I not care, or know how you feel, or be intimately involved with you when My Holy Spirit lives in you?"* **If the Father, Son, and Holy Spirit are One, then how can Father not be intimately involved with the *body* of His Son (*us*) in whom His Spirit dwells?** This would be *impossible*.

During another time, when "storm winds" rushed in on multiple fronts, I was having trouble sleeping one night; my mind was wrestling with a number of sudden changes. I woke up and heard the

Lord say, *"Elroi"*. I immediately thought of the story of Hagar. I got up, opened my Bible, and turned to Genesis 16. There I read about Hagar running away from a painful circumstance. But God put Himself in her path and let her know *"I see what you're going through."*

God revealed Himself to Hagar as *"Elroi"*—*"the God who sees me."* Not only did God let her know that He saw her circumstance, but He gave her counsel, direction, and a promise. These are things God wants us to have as we meet with Him in the midst of our circumstances. God's counsel to her was to go back and submit to the authority over her. Hagar put her trust in God and did as He said.

Father wants us to put our trust in Him and look to Him continually in all things. He will tell us what we need to know and what to do. He sees and cares for us right where we are, using all things to shape our life for His purpose and the divine destiny we carry. His care and power has granted us everything we need for life and godliness regarding the *identity* we carry as His sons and daughters (2 Pet. 1:3).

Papa's Provision

Father supplies unlimited provision *to* us through His Covenant made *with* us in Christ. The legal document of His covenant with us was signed with Jesus' own blood. In God's Word, covenants were a pact, a bond of loyal friendship between two parties. Covenants provided needed supply, aid, and protection—all that one had—for the help and benefit of the other. It even included taking on the debt of the other party as needed. Jesus' blood paid a debt we could never pay, and in Him, we have all provision for every aspect of life *and* godliness.

The book of Psalms contains endless testimony of what God provides for us as His children. Psalm 103 says that He *forgives* all our iniquities, *heals* all our diseases, *redeems* our life from the pit, *crowns* us with lovingkindness, *satisfies* our years with good things, *renews* our strength, *releases* justice for the oppressed, *teaches* us His ways, and does not deal with us according to our sins but *removes* them from us as far as the east is from the west. Psalm 104 continues: He *makes angels His messengers* to us, makes a *way* for us, *sets boundaries*, sends waters to *refresh* and bring *increase*, provides *food*, and sends His Spirit to *renew* the land. That sounds pretty involved if you ask me…and His provision is endless.

Psalm 103:13 says that *as a father has compassion on his children, so the Lord has compassion on those who fear Him.* The word *"compassion"* (Heb. *"racham"*) means: to love deeply with tender affection, to pity, to cherish, to treat gently. Our Father is tender toward us right where we're at in life. He is not stingy, but provides out of the abundance of His grace and kindness for *all* who look to Him, blessing *richly* all who call on Him (Rom. 10:12; Eph. 2:7).

The supply for all our needs comes from Father (Phil. 4:19). He is not indifferent to any of our needs, natural or spiritual. He promises to give supply for our EVERY need out of the vastness of His wealth made available to us *in Christ*. That means that as His sons and daughters, our *source* of provision does not spring *from* the earth realm, but comes from the unseen realm of Father's kingdom (Heb. 11:3). Remember how Jesus supplied food for the multitudes? (Matt. 14:19). Or how God supplied manna in the wilderness? (Exod. 16:15). Remember the wind that made a way for Israel to cross the Red Sea? (Exod. 14:21). Or the earthquake that set Paul and Silas free from the prison house as they were praying and singing praise to God? (Acts 16:25-26) **Father has both unlimited supply** *and* **ways to provide for us.**

God is not a Father who is too busy, distant, distracted, or indifferent regarding our needs. He sees *before* we even ask (Matt. 6:8, 32)! He says, *"Don't worry about what you're going to eat, drink, or wear. I'll take care of you. The very birds of the air eat what I provide through the hands of another. They don't worry; they just accept what I provide and how I provide for them. Aren't you more important to Me than they are? I think you are!"* (Matt. 6:26-28 — personal standard version). **"Fathering" us is what our good Father does.**

Difficult circumstances can make us feel desperate. Father says that if even the wicked know how to give good gifts to their children, how much more will He give good things to those who ask Him, starting with food and shelter (Matt. 7:11). The Father doesn't want us desperate, but deeply dependent on Him, trusting Him for the manifestation of what we need. As we wait for that manifestation, He will give us encouraging words with peace and counsel in the midst of difficulties.

During the time of writing this book, my husband has been out of work for many months. The morning after he received the "pink slip," I woke up with a vision in my spirit as I was just rousing from sleep, though not yet fully awake. Outside, the birds were singing as dawn was breaking. As I lay resting, I had a picture of God *speaking in heaven* and suddenly a small red bird *appeared in the earth realm.* It was quite comical, like something you would see in a cartoon. It was a "poof" moment. I sat up, fully awake, and I knew what God was saying. **He was letting me know that the manifestation of our provision would come from the unseen realm of heaven into the seen realm of the earth.** Our expectation was to be in Him and His Word.

Father has both natural and spiritual provision for us. He has riches that strengthen us in spirit, soul, and body in the midst of *every* situation (Eph. 3:16). Jesus said that we don't live by bread *alone*, but by every word that comes from the mouth of God. He will supply natural bread, but He also has *true* bread (Matt. 4:4; John 6:32). Like a baby chick completely dependent on what comes from mama bird's mouth, we are dependent on Father's Word for all of life.

Father's full provision comes from the unseen realm of spiritual blessing in heavenly places. It manifests in our life as finances, food, employment, and shelter, as well as wisdom and revelation. There is no separation of natural versus spiritual with Him. We are spirit *and* natural beings. He cares about *all* of who we are: spirit, soul, and body. When we minister the power and love of God to people, it must include the whole man. Our *whole* life is valuable to God. Scripture says that if our Father pays attention to even the smallest sparrow that falls to the ground—whose worth cannot be compared to ours—how much more valuable is our life to Him? He sees us. He sees our need. And He cares (Matt. 10:29; 18:14).

Father has given us an eternal hope and *expectation* by which our heart can be strengthened in all things (2 Thess. 2:16, 17). His divine provision has made us *qualified* to share in a great inheritance *in* light (Col. 1:12). His work in us through the Spirit and the Son, *qualifies* us (makes us *suitable*) for eternal glory! His provision of grace makes us *suitable* heirs through fellowship with one Father *from* whom all things come, one Lord *through* whom all things come, and one Spirit *by* whom all things come (1 Cor. 8:6).

Papa is a *Safe* Place

Our Heavenly Father is not only good to provide for us, but He is a *safe* Father. Psalm 78:53 says, "He led them **safely**, so that they did not fear; but the sea engulfed their enemies" (emphasis mine). Our Father doesn't treat us harshly or go into a rage when we do something wrong. He doesn't beat His children. That is not His nature. His own description of Himself (that is true, unlike the descriptions some give Him which are not true) is that He is gentle, long-suffering, compassionate, gracious, slow to anger, is rich in kindness and truth, and forgives sin and offenses. He is *overflowing* with lovingkindness (Exod. 34:6-7; Ps. 103:8). However, He does say that the guilty would not go unpunished. He is a **righteous Father**. That was what Jesus called Him (John 17:25). All His actions toward us are *righteous*.

While Father *is* firm and does correct us, He does so in *love*, not in anger. In fact, as the Father of all, He instructs all earthly fathers to discipline their children, but *never* in anger (Eph. 6:4). Unsafe actions of earthly parents—especially in the area of discipline—are one of the biggest influences that make us feel unsafe with God before we come to truly know Him. You know—"*the lightening is going to strike*" mentality. While we laugh in using that cliché, it is a subtle mindset many embrace. We fear discipline because we probably grew up not being rightly disciplined in love. We were only punished. Or maybe it was a mixture of both and we never knew what was coming. A parent may love a child, but unsafe discipline sends another message.

Fear promotes a feeling of being *unsafe*. While we *are* to fear God and tremble at His Word, that kind of fear is rooted in reverence and love that runs *to* Him to be safe. Holy fear encourages us to draw near to God, knowing that He loves us and is bigger than any enemy or difficulty we face. **Our Father is supremely great,**

and yet intrinsically kind. He stoops low to help us. As we trust His care, *unrighteous* fear is removed. **Even when our world is shaken, confidence in His love makes us know we are safe.** Fear, worry, and anxiety operate *apart* from love, but fear is *driven out* by the presence of love (1 John 4:18). If we feel unsafe, then we need to ask why.

Though there is a *day of wrath* coming of judgment on the wicked, His judgment is righteous and *forewarned.* There *is* a righteous anger of God, and believe me, He can be violent against His enemies. But He is not impulsive, moody, or uncontrolled, nor does He act in fist-flailing hostility, especially toward His children. He is not a brawler, He doesn't act rashly or rude, nor does He discipline as such. Slapping, yelling, and name calling to change another's behavior is a destructive reality in many homes. This is not Father's way. It is not honorable. It is not love. It does not produce righteousness, and teaches a child that the home is unsafe and that discipline has no purpose other than to inflict punishment, or release one's own anger and frustration. That is how man acts, not God. Father's hands are safe hands.

While God *is* a Man of War, He is not a "violent man". What's the difference? As a Man of War, God fights for what is right and upholds justice; a violent man is one who rages against others out of wickedness and an evil heart. As a Man of War, Father protects what is His—**we are His!** Dad fights for us and shows Himself strong on the behalf of those who love Him (Deut. 1:30-32). That's what the cross was all about. We see the Father's nature to fight and rescue what belongs to Him through the lives of His sons, too, such as Abraham and David (read Genesis 14:14-16 and 1 Samuel 30:8-18). **When we know our Father's thoughts and nature toward us, we will live from that reality and perspective.**

Jesus trusted the Father implicitly. If He hadn't, He wouldn't have been able to drink the cup of suffering. In the midst of many unsafe circumstances, our Elder Brother was confident in the safety of Abba's nearness—Father's *safe* love filled Him. He knew that if He asked, Father would have sent twelve legions of angels to save Him, but He didn't ask (Mat. 26:53). Trusting the Father's love in the midst of pain kept Jesus *staying the course* without wavering.

How often do we drink a "cup of suffering" without wavering? Or suffer some injustice without hurting someone else out of our own pain? We may not understand the "why" of difficulties we go through or delays to answers, but Father wants us to trust Him. He will carry us *through* impossibilities, wildernesses, places of bitter water, times of great need, and stormy seasons. He will refresh us with the rain of His presence when we are dry and weary, and He will bring us *out* into larger realms and plant us on higher places (Ps. 68:9).

Joy and having a good sense of humor also helps to refuse negative thoughts sent by the enemy to promote unsafe feelings. Father Himself must have a great sense of humor because in His presence is *complete joy* and pleasures that last forever (Ps. 16:11). God is holy—not gloomy. There is an unexplainable intrinsic pleasure and delight in God's presence that ***satisfies*** the heart and soul. Man seeks thrills, adventure, drama, and excitement through many means, but those are temporal pleasures. God's abiding presence satisfies the whole man—spirit, soul, and body—with a deep and *eternal* delight.

The nature of the Holy Spirit is also joy (Gal. 5:22). Jesus Himself was anointed with joy (Heb. 1:9). **So there we have it—the Godhead is a joyful God!** I have seen people be so overwhelmed by the presence of God's joy it was as if they were drunk. I have experienced it myself!

The early church began with 120 people experiencing that same joy as they were baptized in the Holy Spirit and fire. God's joy in them was so strong that people thought they were drunk as they came out of the Upper Room and into the streets of Jerusalem proclaiming the testimony of Jesus (Acts 2). God is a God of joy and He wants us to be joyful. I once had a pastor tell me that God doesn't want people happy, just faithful. I don't attend his church anymore! Why would a joyful God not want a joyful people? God commands us to be joyful! Psalm 89:15 says, *"How blessed are the people who know the joyful sound! O Lord, they walk in the light of Your countenance."* Isaiah 64:5 says that God *meets* with him who *rejoices* and does righteousness. He says His people REJOICE ALL DAY IN HIS NAME! (Ps. 89:16). As a parent, I want my kids to be joyful, not gloomy!

As sons and daughters of God we have been given the mind of our Elder Brother which is one that is joyful and peaceful (1 Cor. 2:16). What does a reality check of our thoughts say? What is our perception of our circumstances, God, or others? What is the state of our heart in trying times? Is it gloomy? Fearful? Or is it joyful expectation? When we are filled with God's joy, we feel safe. His joy is our strength (Neh. 8:10).

Father Keeps His Promises

Some people are "slackers" regarding their words, but Father is not (2 Pet. 3:9). He makes promises that He keeps. Most everyone has been impacted by unfulfilled promises made by earthly parents, but our Father actually *watches over His Word to perform it* (Jer. 1:12). His own zeal accomplishes His Word! (Isa. 9:7). However, the fulfillment of His promises is also often linked with our obedience (Jer. 11:4-5). While we may have to wait patiently for Father's promises to be fulfilled, His timing is perfect. Meanwhile, He wants us to enjoy the journey with Him and understand that He is a Father who *loves processes*. He is always working something out. Father enjoys the journey with us because He knows our end from the beginning.

As we listen and do what He tells us, He will do the rest (Luke 24:49). Meanwhile, He is working in multiple ways, on multiple fronts, preparing us for the fulfillment of His Word.

God is sovereign in *how* He fulfills His Word. Too many times we expect Father to fulfill His promises exactly how *we* think it should happen. But look at a dream that Joseph had of his father, mother, and eleven brothers all bowing down to him (Gen. 37:9-10). The reality was that Joseph's mother had already died when his prophetic dream came to pass. But the purpose of the dream wasn't about her, but about God's plan for Joseph and how he would become a ruler and provider for many, including his family. She was part of his family. When we expect Father's words to play out according to our own interpretation, we set ourselves up for disillusionment, discouragement, and unfulfilled expectations. All of God's promises are "yes and amen," but we must also let Him work them out the way He wants to. <u>Our expectation then becomes God</u>

<u>Himself and His Word, not the circumstances</u>. Father is faithful and He will perform all His good work (Phil. 1:6). Fulfillment of promises may not always look like what we think, but with God, it will always be good!

Dad *Actively* Listens

One of the most important tools of good parenting is good listening. While parents often ask their children, "Did you hear me?" they themselves often have a *listening* problem. Our Heavenly Father does not. He has the keenest listening skills—He hears even when we don't want Him to... like when we're complaining! He hears our thoughts before we even speak. He hears our cries and prayers and He answers us (Ps. 65:2).

Earthly parents are often inattentive and "tune-out" the kids. "Tune-out" means the kids are speaking on one frequency and we have turned the dial and cannot hear them. When children are small, it is easy to "tune-them-out" with all their chatter, endless questions, and "I wants". At nine and ten years old, my two children realized my practice of tuning-them-out and made a game of it. They would come and stand beside me while I was reading and make comments like, "We're going to take the car and drive to Disneyworld now." They wanted to see if I was listening to their plans of making a 900 mile trip on their own ... in my car! If I was studying, or lost in thought, I would respond, "Uh-huh, okay, that's fine." Then they would burst out laughing. I would "wake-up" from my thoughts and laugh with them, too.

While we may smile at that scenario, many times the "tune-out" habit becomes a lack of awareness as to what is really going on with our children. Being *unaware* means lack of action. But our Father who says to watch and pray is Himself *always* alert to us. People may tune us out, but Father God does not tune us out. He is always watchful and attentively listens. **He not only seeks to hear and understand, He *does* hear and understand.** He hears our words, our thoughts, our desires, and our pain. He listens. He sees. He answers.

Our Father actively listens to us:

- He hears our grieving (Jer. 31:8)
- He hears our prayers and sees our tears (2 Kings 20:5)
- He hears our groaning in bondage (Exod. 6:5)
- He hears our cry for help (2 Sam. 22:7)
- He hears our words (Dan. 10:12)
- He also hears our complaining (Exod. 16:12)

Remember, Father's eyes look continually throughout the whole earth to show Himself strong on behalf of those whose heart is *completely His*. King David lived in the confidence of knowing that God heard his prayers. Therefore he sought God's counsel and help continually *with* expectation of His response (Ps. 40:1; 116:2). Father God wants us to live in the confidence that He is attentive to us, and that when we ask, He will answer. He says, "**Ask, and it *will* be given you; seek and you *will* find; knock, and it *will* be opened to you**" (Matt. 7:7, emphasis mine).

As children, we need to have patience. However, it is also frustrating when we feel we are not heard, or are not listened to. Though we cannot always help how others respond to us, we must be careful not to let feelings of having *no voice* translate into our relationship with God. God is not a man and we must not treat Him as such. If we are waiting for some needed answer, there is a reason. Keep confident and keep in prayer. Sometimes He doesn't always tell us *why* at the moment, but He *is* a good Father and will speak to us. He will also work things out as we pray and look to Him for the answer to our needs.

Jesus taught those who followed Him to be confident in the Father's involvement with them saying, *"Whatever you ask in the Son's name, Father will give it to you"* (John 16:23). The Apostle John said, *"This is the confidence which we have before Him, that if we ask anything according to His will, He hears us. And if we know that He hears us in whatever we ask, we know that we have the requests which we have asked from Him"* (1 John 5:14-15). God also gives a specific promise that we are heard when two are in prayerful agreement regarding His will (Matt. 18:19).

There are some things that aide our ability to receive answers from Father:

- All things are possible to him who prays and *believes* (Matt. 21:22; Mark 11:24)
- *Abiding* in Jesus and His Words (John 15:7)
- Walking in *forgiveness* (Mark 11:25-26)
- *Asking*! (James 4:2)
- Asking with *right motives* (James 4:3)
- Praying according to *His will* (1 John 5:14-15)
- Treating our *spouse with love* (1 Pet. 3:7)

Jesus was confident that Father *always* heard Him (John 11:41-42). Jesus didn't say that Father jumped to answer Him, but He knew that Father always actively heard Him and would answer. And so, Jesus thanked Him before He saw the answer appear. Practicing gratitude for all Father *has* done helps keep our heart in a place of faith while we wait on His perfect timing for answers. Complaining about what Father *hasn't* done doesn't make Him hear us any better—at least not in a good way . . . just a thought.

It grieves a parent who works hard and seeks the well-being of their child to receive expressions of that child's distrust in their care or disbelief in their words. While parents are imperfect and may give cause to some mistrust, whining is rooted in a child's self-centeredness. Whining at God is self-centered as it casts a shadow on His motives, desire, and ability to care for us. Godly faith is God-centered. I'm sure we've all whined at God at one time or another, but whining grieves Him. Immersing our prayers and petitions with gratitude toward Father honors Him (1 Thess. 5:18).

Cultivating a lifestyle of praise and thanksgiving is an expression of trust that Father is *actively* listening and cares.

Actively Listening to Dad!

Now it's *our* turn to listen. Like all children, one of our greatest needs as sons and daughters of God is cultivating the skill of learning to listen to God. You know—put down the book, turn off the T.V., hang up the phone, do the dishes later, stop complaining, and leave the computer alone while we listen to what Father is saying to us. After all, He *is* more important, isn't He?

When we are born-again, we come as a child into a kingdom—one that has a whole new culture and new way of doing things. Previously, we may have cultivated a lifestyle of not listening well to anyone! But now, dull hearing and pretend listening have to be thrown out and replaced with ears that pay attention to Father's words. It is both a mark of maturity and a victory over *self* when we, as children, learn to listen to Father's instructions… and *do* them. No, you can't skip this section of the book.

The impact that good instruction produces in our life is dependent on a tender heart that listens to the Father, Son, and Holy Spirit: a tender heart *plus* a listening ear establishes a life of faith and thus one of power. Our instruction as His children is so important, that God wrote a whole book specifically on the importance of *listening* to instruction. It's called the book of Proverbs. There we read of how Wisdom is like a woman who stands at the top of the street calling to us, *"Listen to Me and you shall live!"* Listening is an important theme with God and He repeatedly says, *"He that has ears to hear, let him hear"* (Matt. 11:15).

When we were born-again, we were given *spiritual* senses of sight, hearing, discernment, touch, and speech. **We have been given ears to hear God, but listening is a choice.** And even when we listen, there are different *ways* we listen:

- *Passive listening* (we hear but do not obey, or delay obedience)
- *Selective listening* (we listen with *bias* or for what we *want* to hear)
- *Inattentive listening* (we focus in and out of the conversation)
- *Attentive listening* (we seek to hear and understand, and *take action*)

Father wants us to *attentively listen* to Him, just as He actively listens to us. Any other form of listening, is *not* listening.

Father's Instructions

The Word of God is our foundation of instruction from Father. It teaches us about His character, ways, and purpose. While God instructs us through His written *and* spoken Word, His **voice** will *always* be consistent with His written *Word*. We need to know His written Word intimately so that we are sure if what we hear in our *inner man* or thoughts is consistent with God's nature and purpose, or not. Following voices and thoughts that are contrary to the Word of God is what leads us into all kinds of error. *Attentive* listening to His voice keeps us from listening to or following other voices.

What are some of the ways that God speaks to us other than His written Word? A word we hear in our spirit-man, impressions, a sense of knowing something, feelings, even colors and smells are a way He speaks to us. He uses people, parents, friends, leaders, circumstances, books, dreams, visions, creation, *His* angels, etc. God speaks to us in endless ways, but again, ***always consistent with His written Word.*** Jesus said that His sheep hear (listen to) His voice, He knows them, and they follow Him (John 10:27). Jesus only spoke what He heard from Father, so listening to Jesus is also listening to Father. The Son speaks the Father's words. The Holy Spirit also speaks (John 16:13). ***God is a speaking God.*** The question is: what is He saying to you? What is He saying to me? Are we listening?

All of God's instructions give life. To sum them up—as Jesus did—would be the instruction to love. **Listening is an act of love.**

> "You shall love the Lord your God with all your heart,
> and with all your soul,
> and with all your strength, and with all your mind, and your neighbor as yourself"
> Luke 10:27

According to Father, listening is only completed by *doing*. If we don't *do* what we hear, then we haven't really heard. And if we don't listen and do, then we don't really love. Pleasures, self-will, and distractions are all things that a child must be trained to esteem **less important** than a parent's instruction. It is the same for us regarding Father's voice. Esteeming self-centeredness above Father's words is what plummeted mankind into darkness—you know—the place we have been translated *out of.*

The success of our development as sons and daughters of God rests on love that listens to and follows divine instruction. Listening with obedience to authority is an act of selflessness. Parents often ignorantly cultivate the self-centered nature of their child through over permissiveness, and allowing the child to "call the shots." For example, I was one of those parents who too often allowed my children to finish what they were doing before making them obey some task I had assigned. I was trying to find the "balance" of discipline yet without being overly controlling. However, I didn't realize what they were actually learning. I was teaching them that *they* were *greater than me*. And we all know the saying: "give 'em an inch and they'll take a mile". Their *"just a minute"* became *"later,"* and *"later"* became *"tomorrow."* And tomorrow never comes.

How often do we do that with Father God? Are we acting on what He is saying? Or do we say, *"Just a minute"*? Who do our actions show to be the most important one in our life? Us or our Father?

Catering to a child's own timetable results in establishing the hierarchy of a child's will as supreme. A supreme self-will is an unbending tyrant . . . a wild tail that tries to wag the dog. We do not "wag" Father, and He does not cater to our whims. While God, as a parent, does not act with impulsive anger, He does move in truth, love, and firmness so that we learn to regard His voice as more important than anything else. If we don't, we are the loser for **there is nothing that robs us more of victory and destiny than self-will.**

Sometimes it is not blatant sin or self-will, but the voice of our circumstance, loss, or emotional turmoil that keeps us from hearing Father. Peace is important for the health of our soul and ability to receive direction from God. **Peace is the ambient in which we best hear Father's voice and receive divine revelation.** No wonder Father sent Jesus as the Prince of Peace. Satan works to keep us out of peace, but keeping our mind stayed on God and trusting Him in all things keeps us in perfect peace (Isa. 26:3). 1 Pet. 3:11 says to seek peace and *pursue* it! Run after it! Make it a priority for the health and wholeness of your thought life.

What is the voice you are hearing right now? Your own? The enemy? Circumstances? Truth? It is important to discern what we are hearing. Only then can we capture wrong thoughts and bring them into the obedience of the knowledge of God and His truth. The world, the flesh, and the devil whisper lies in our ears; their words produce death (John 8:38, 44). Father's voice produces life and His instruction leads us in wisdom and righteousness that produce joy.

God's Word tells us that a child who refuses instruction reaps personal destruction and curses (afflictions, condemnation, and evil) upon their life (Proverbs). That is *not* joy. He says that lightly esteeming [*dishonoring, disgracing, or treating shamefully*] a parent's instructions reaps *curses*. One day that child will say, *"Woe is me because I have hated instruction and spurned my teachers"* (Deut. 27:16; Prov. 5). How much more important then is it to embrace Father God's instructions that impact our eternity?

The Holy Spirit is given to us as a Teacher for a divine purpose. God says that embracing instruction and wisdom brings *blessing* on our life, both present and eternal. Proverbs 4:9 says that wisdom crowns us with honor as when someone wins an Olympic game! We are running the race of life and Father wants us to go for the *gold*! He honors the one who honors Him and His Words.

Receiving Father's Counsel

What is the difference between instruction and counsel? By definition, *instruction* is information, teaching, and knowledge given as direction or command; *counsel* is instruction, but is also recommendation given upon request or as an exhortation or warning. We tend to seek counsel when we need advice in a specific circumstance. We ask, *"Dad, what do I do now, in this moment of time?"* But Father wants us to request His counsel daily. His counsel will satisfy us in times of drought and make us like a flourishing garden with a spring that never goes dry (Isa. 58:11).

God's counsel sees areas in us where we are blind and lack understanding. In Revelation 3:18, Jesus *counseled* the church of Laodicea to buy of Him gold that is tried in the fire. They looked "fine" on the outside, but their heart was not right and they needed *counsel* to save them from possible judgment. In the Old Testament, too, one of Father God's greatest issues with His son, Israel, was their waywardness as *a nation lacking in counsel and without understanding.*

Living without godly instruction *and* daily divine counsel promotes choices made apart from the wisdom of God. This causes a lack of understanding and inability to discern our future (Deut. 32:28-29). God wants us have divine insight for the present and future! He wants us to be a people who know the hour of our visitation and the seasons of God so that we move with Him. He also wants us to know the timing of judgment so that we also move with Him accordingly.

Israel knew how to stand before earthly fathers to honor them, but neglected to do so with Father God. They were created to be a nation of priests who ministered to God, but their heart waned with desire to be like the rest of the nations and thus, served their gods. They rejected knowledge, so blindness masked any discernment about what future awaits those who forget God. Worldly pursuit made them ignorant and unwise. **Seeking God's counsel makes us wise and enables us to *see* the future.**

However, God didn't forsake Israel, but continually called them to return from their waywardness and know their destiny. Father calls us to come out of our waywardness, as well. As His children, we are not to be like the rest of the nations. We are a people created for Him. Psalm 32:8 reads (Amplified Bible), "*I will instruct [give insight to] you and teach you in the way which you should go; I will counsel [advise, purpose] you with My eye upon you.*" As the body of Christ, we have been given the ***Spirit of Counsel***. When we turn a deaf ear to Father, we are quenching His Spirit. While God does not forsake His children, He does say that His Spirit will not always *strive* with man (Gen. 6:3).

If we are in relationship with someone and our actions are grieving them, we need to examine our heart, and most especially so in our relationship with God. I am eternally grateful for God's patience with me, but He has better plans for me, and for you, than to always be calling us back from waywardness. He wants us to move forward into His promises. He has a land of inheritance for us to possess. He wants us to run after *Him*, not the world! (Song of Sol. 1:4). He has a glorious future and a present plan for us, and it can only be known through seeking His counsel.

Proverbs 8:34 says, "Blessed is the man who listens to Me, watching daily at My gates." 2 Chron. 29:11 says, "My sons, do not be negligent now, for the LORD has chosen you to stand before Him, to minister to Him, and to be His ministers and burn incense." That incense represents prayer and intercession. We are called to be *priests* unto God who wait on Him continually (Rev. 1:6). A lifestyle of priesthood is one that is dedicated to prayer and intimacy with God. As we draw near to Him, He promises to meet with us and give us His counsel (Exod. 30:6).

Proverbs 8:14-15 says that **counsel is found in the fear of the Lord** and **by it kings reign**. *We are kings* who have been appointed a kingdom (Luke 22:29). God's counsel makes us prosperous and victorious in battle (Judg. 18:5; 20:18, 23). When we get Father's counsel and declare it into our home, business, or other sphere of influence, we release divine power from heaven into the earth realm. God's voice shakes the heavens and earth. When heaven shifts by the voice of God, earth moves. Satan works to distract us from listening to God because He knows that God's counsel is *our* victory and *his* defeat.

In the New Testament, Paul also speaks of our Heavenly Father as One who counsels us regarding His purposes and our future, showing us the way we should go (1 Thess. 3:11). Many voices try to "counsel" us including fear, our flesh, and the *appearance* of circumstances. But Father wants us to listen to His counsel no matter what our eyes see.

We are in the last days and there is a great shaking already beginning in the earth. Nation will rise against nation and natural disasters will increase. Persecution and offenses will abound and cultures will be in tumult. Gross darkness and deception will cover the earth, and people will fear. Scripture says that people will be lovers of themselves and of money; they will be proud, disobedient, ungrateful, unholy, unloving, and loving pleasure rather than loving God. They will hold to a form of religion that has no power (Matt. 24; 2 Tim. 3:1-7; Isa. 60:2). But something else has also been promised for the last days: the outpouring of His Holy Spirit upon His sons and daughters. God's children will see visions, dream dreams and prophesy (Acts 2:17; Hab. 2:14). They will move in the *power of His presence* and His counsel and do exploits. His glory will be on His people who love Him and who take confident refuge in Him, not in the world (Prov. 14:26).

As sons and daughters of God, we must break every *inward* tie to worldly systems and be governed by the counsel of God. Our thinking must be rooted in the kingdom of heaven, not in the kingdoms of this world. As we seek His counsel, Father will show us what we are to do. In the Old Testament, His people prospered even in times of famine and judgment as long as they *listened* to Him and *loved* Him, not idols.

Agreement with the Word of God

Our words carry power. Psalm 19:14 says, "Let the words of my mouth, and the meditation of my heart, be acceptable in Your sight, O Lord, my Rock and my Redeemer." Agreement with God's counsel begins with agreement with His Word.

The following declarations are ways to practice (aloud) agreement with God and right meditation as His sons and daughters. These cultivate peace in our inner man:

- I am God's child: a new creation in Christ.
- I am loved by Father God.
- Father provides all that I need.
- The Heavenly Father is actively involved in my life.
- I am safe in the Father's love.
- I am valuable to Abba Father; I am the apple of His eye.
- As I look to God, I have peace.
- Father's counsel makes me victorious.
- The Word of God nurtures me.
- My Father watches over His promises to perform them.
- Father God is compassionate and gracious with me.
- I am joyful because Father's presence is always with me.

Personal Application:

1. In what ways do you see Father's provision in your life?
2. Do you see Father God as safe? Why or why not?
3. What are some of Father's promises to you?
4. Do you feel like Father listens to you?
5. Do you feel like you listen to Father?
6. What was the last counsel Father gave you? Did you act on His counsel?

CHAPTER 8

Dad's Discipline

A parent's task is to *see* the future that a child does not see and prepare them for it through discipline. Many people, even Christians, wander through life because they have no vision. They do not see divine purpose for their life and so live undisciplined. But the Father sees our destiny, as well as the heart and ways *within us* that prevent the fullness of His plans from being accomplished *through us.* Father sees our end from our beginning and thus disciplines us with *present* and *eternal* purpose in mind.

Engaging a disciplined life shapes who we are. Proverbs 22:15 says that *foolishness* **is bound up in the heart of a child, but the** *rod of discipline* **removes it.** Foolishness in the heart disregards God and His ways. In Scripture, a *"rod"* is seen as a symbol of authority, correction, or as an instrument (a standard) by which something is measured (Ezek. 40:3; Rev. 11:1). The Father's rod of discipline is a *golden* rod; gold speaks of that which is pure and without mixture, and what is divine rather than earthly. His golden rod drives out the earthly foolishness and mixture from our heart. His discipline measures our character against the pattern of Christ's image, as His standard of love assesses our thoughts, motives, and ways. Father has our destiny in view!

Foolishness is rooted in the self-life that stands, as a child, on the top of a hill declaring, "*I* am king!" As "king," the self-life makes its choices based on its own desires, but the end of that path is destruction (Prov. 14:12). No parent wants to see their child end in ruin. How much more Father God? Look at the price He has already paid to save us from eternal death. The Father's discipline is the expression of His love working to save us from ourselves; He returns our wayward heart so that we declare, "*He* is King!" His discipline works to remove us from our own little exalted place as He forms us into His humble, yet mighty, sons and daughters.

Father God uses His rod of discipline to *free us* from the deception of a self-imposed *counterfeit* authority. The result of discipline equips us to be able to rightly handle the rod of His *true* authority. **Thus, the rod of divine discipline becomes the rod of divine authority in our life.**

Discipline and Character

Father's discipline includes instruction, chastening, and correction. Although the word *discipline* (Heb. "*muwcar*") carries an understanding of inflicting pain, it is *not* as hostile aggression, but as *striking* the heart of self-centeredness. Father's discipline captures our attention where we have ignored His law of love, and works to bring us back into harmony with Himself. His discipline works to remove sin from our heart and error from our ways. **He chastens us as a means to cultivate both mind and morals, removing anything not in alignment with *His* character.** He admonishes and rebukes us in order to curb unholy passions. His discipline even includes the care of the body; He cares about *every* aspect of our life! He cares how we treat our body, seeing that we can't fulfill His purposes if we destroy our body through abuses and unrighteous lifestyles.

Discipline is a critical part of our character development, for right character is vital to a life of victory. Character is defined as the attributes that distinguish who we are. Character is the government of the *inner man*—the soul, thoughts, emotions, and will—

which is expressed through *outward* behavior, conduct, and choice. Right character is what makes a person truly successful—not talents, money, positions, or an easy life. Godly character brings divine favor in God's time for appointed places.

Father wants *His* character to be the government of our inner man. He wants *His* character to govern not just *what* we do, but *why* we do it, because of *who* we are as His heirs. Agreement with carnal mindsets and ungodly reasoning hold us in a place of powerlessness. But we were born of God to rule with power! The Holy Spirit, who abides in our spirit man, wants to move and be active, but our agreement with sin quenches His movement. Continuing in ways of the flesh learned when we were in darkness renders our spirit man powerless. Father disciplines us to remove those carnal attitudes and replace them with righteous mindsets that *empower* our spirit man to rule by the Spirit rather than being ruled by the soul (mind, will, emotions).

For some, the thought of discipline brings back negative memories. As children, discipline may have been inconsistent, excessive, or in anger. Its purpose may have seemed more of a way for the parent to vent frustration or even rage. That is not discipline and it does not save a child from himself. It can even cause deep hurt and turmoil. Father God does not discipline us like that. As we read previously, the Father instructs earthly fathers to *not* correct a child in anger or in a way that *dis*courages the child.

Right discipline not only roots out error, but works to *promote courage* in us to do what is right. Father's discipline works to *empower* us toward right action which results in a life of power. No flesh likes discipline in the moment, but when we humbly embrace it, it produces a harvest of righteousness and peace (Heb. 12:11). **A humble heart embraces discipline because it discerns God's purpose in the midst of discipline.**

Even Job (who suffered afflictions we'd prefer not to experience!) said, *"Behold, how happy is the man whom God reproves, so do not despise the discipline of the Almighty"* (Job 5:17). Job walked through suffering, but came out with a double portion. However, as joyous as it was to receive double for all that had been lost, the greatest thing Job gained through that season was that he saw God.

Affliction exposed Job's heart, but also gave him a greater knowledge of the Most High. Revelation of God through discipline brings inward transformation.

The Father uses many ways to discipline us including people and circumstances. Like a Refiner of gold, He uses *affliction* to purify us. He engages the fires of life to bring the dross within us to the surface in order to remove it. He works until He sees the reflection of Himself in the gold. As we turn to Him, He will reveal truth to bring inward change. The result of His work is deep inward joy, though it may not feel joyful at the time. **The joy begins when we realize we are being disciplined** *because we are loved.*

The Narrow Way of Royalty

Proverbs 22:6 says, *"Train up a child in the way he should go, even when he is old he will not depart from it."* The Hebrew word *"train"* (*"chanak"*) means: to make narrow. The word *"narrow"* (Grk. *"stenos"*) means: to groan, running counter to natural inclinations. It means: to *press* as with affliction. The Father's discipline is part of His training in our life. He is not raising us as ordinary children, but as ***kings and priests*** (Rev. 1:6). These two positions carry governmental authority and both require specific discipline *and* training. The chief thing about kings and priests is that they are positions of ***power and influence*** with God and man. Both are positions that release blessing for the prosperity of a people group or nation (we will read more about the blessing later).

The discipline of God's training presses against our *natural* inclinations. God "presses" us in order to break away the hard shell of the *natural* or *carnal* life that hinders us. "Brokenness" allows the movement of the indwelling Holy Spirit to be released like oil poured out. In the Bible, God's people are referred to as an olive tree. An olive *press* is an instrument designed to *crush* the olive so that oil is released. Oil, in Scripture, is used for healing and anointing. Jesus went through the olive press for the healing of mankind. As Abba Father's children, there is an abiding anointing of His Spirit in us that wants released for the healing of the nations.

Our calling in God is specific and our training narrow. **We all like the thought of having power and influence, but are we willing to go through the process that will purge out the self-centeredness that propagates corruption in places of power?** At the time of this writing, the economy of our nation is being shaken because of corruption in high places. But that self-centeredness isn't just in men of places in power, but is in every one of us. We may not see it, but Father does. He works to remove it so that *His* power can flow through us in purity and we not become corrupt with pride and greed. Corruption causes not only our fall, but as our life impacts others, our fall also hurts others.

We have seen this not only in the world, but in ministries throughout the body of Christ. Even as Christians, we can be self-centered and our ministry self-serving. Self-serving operates as the hand that secretly *takes* as it appears to give. We can look good on the outside, but inside our motives and thoughts may be unholy. We see it and don't like it. Sometimes we try to ignore it or deny it. But it's there and hinders our ability to fully love God and others. It taints the Father's work through us and quenches the voice of the Spirit in us. But Father doesn't ignore it. He loves us, so He works to remove the nature of self that defiles us. His discipline is an *expression of His love* and *delight* in us (Prov. 3:12). He knows that our ways lead to death—no matter how good they look!

When we give our life to God, He takes our hand and leads us on the *narrow way*. That way is the *way of the cross*. The cross puts to death worldly ways that hinder us from love. The cross puts to death the old so that the new man can be raised in *power* to live as Father's heritage in the earth. The cross breaks off the crust of sin and self so that the anointed man within us is free to move with the Spirit.

Disciplined for Destiny

As Son of Man, Jesus, too, had to *learn* obedience through the things He suffered (Heb. 5:8). **He chose the *narrow* way, teaching it as the *only* way to life.** He also taught that the *wide* way is the way to destruction (Matt. 7:13-14). **Today, He sits on the throne with Father.**

Jesus did not come clothed in His glory as Son of God, but He came as *humble* Son of Man, taking on our form and flesh. Knowing He had a divine purpose to fulfill, He allowed the Father to discipline and train Him through suffering, rejection, years of silent labor, and the pressures of life. He allowed Father's perfect timing to order His steps. Submission to discipline matured His life as a *true* Son. Submission to discipline shaped His life as one that was led, unhindered, by the Spirit into a *fulfilled* destiny—a life that impacted the whole world, and worlds to come, forever.

Father has a destiny for us to walk in, too. His discipline trains us *specifically* for who we are. James 4:7 says we are to *submit to God and resist the devil.* The word *"submit"* (Grk. *"hypotasso"*) means: to yield to another's command or admonition; to be subject to another with obedience. The term "submit" was also a Greek military term meaning "to arrange troop divisions in a military fashion." Submission is not about "control," but about yielding in obedience to a Commander for the purpose of training and arranging us as troops! Submission means to have a *sub mission* under a higher authority. We are the army of God and each one has a calling that requires training for a divine mission. We don't choose our own mission, nor do we do our own thing for God. But then, neither is submission to discipline about being a doormat.

Submission is about being **trained through honor to authority that cultivates the ability to carry authority and be sent out** for the Father's purpose. We are Father's troops who He sends to establish His kingdom in the earth No commander sends an untrained troop into combat. It would mean their death as well as a failed mission. Father loves you and wants you to live. He also has a mission for you to accomplish.

Submission to Father's discipline matures us to **move with eternity with an eternal kingdom.** We don't get those results on the *"wide"* way. Father is raising us as *trained* heirs to govern with His government of divine love. In Chapter 1, we learned that a father is one who brings forth those who are **animated with the same spirit as himself.** So it is with Abba Father. He disciplines, chastens and corrects to shape us into the same character as Himself. He works to bring us into one mind with Him *so that our entire life is animated with the same Spirit as Himself.*

We are the Father's "arrows" prepared in the hidden place of His quiver. He sends us, not randomly, but as *"polished"* arrows who will not miss the mark (Isa. 49:2). A *"polished"* arrow is one that is shaped, cleaned, and proven through testing, able to fly to its designated target and accomplish the Heavenly Archer's purpose. Father is polishing you as a unique arrow and has a specific target for you to hit.

Proverbs 13:18 says that *without discipline* we come to poverty and shame—that is not our Father's target! His target is abundance and glory. **Father God wants to transform what is *in* us so that we are able to go the *way* He sends us.** He has a world to touch, heal, and govern through us.

Removing Every Spot and Wrinkle

While God has given us the metaphor of family to help us understand who He is and our relationship with Him, there is another picture of relationship in God's Word that I have not yet touched on in this book—that is the picture of us as the *bride of Christ*. A bride is one who is presented in garments of pure white to the one she loves. Father is preparing a people who are of *like nature* with His Son and are wholly devoted to Him. These will reign with Him forever. To be prepared means that every spot of sin and wrinkle of self must be removed. Jesus was the Lamb *without spot*; we are being conformed to *His* likeness as a people without spot or wrinkle (1 Pet. 1:19; Eph. 5:27).

Father works diligently with us, that we be *holy* and *blameless* in love for His Son's return (Eph. 1:4). Jesus didn't only call God *"Abba Father,"* He also called Him *"**Holy Father**"* (John 17:11). Seeing Father's holiness makes the blood of Jesus precious to us for the washing away of every sin, and His discipline to be desired for the removing of every wrinkle.

Satan doesn't want us to be a bride prepared or a people who rule with Christ. He wants this world for himself. He knows the rod of divine authority we hold is gold, and he is a seeker of gold. However he doesn't buy gold, he *steals* it because he is a thief (John 10:10). He doesn't waste time on worthless things; he seeks treasure. We are God's treasure and the life of God in us is pure gold. Satan hunts for the precious life within, cunningly working to steal the gold of a pure mind and loving heart. His scheme from the beginning has never changed; he wants to depose man from our place of authority, thus he works to defile us so he can gloat over us (Micah 4:11-13).

Father's discipline *teaches* us to discern the schemes of the enemy and the voice of the flesh that lay snares that pull us into mindsets apart from the intimate knowledge of God and His love. Father makes us wise as serpents yet gentle as doves (Matt. 10:16). He has given us *authority* to tread on serpents (Luke 10:19).

Discipline brings us *closer* to God. When we willingly embrace His chastening, we will find His presence near. If we ever feel a separation from Him, it may be that we are the one who is being stubborn, or offended. If we feel any separation, we can ask Him why. He will tell us.

Honoring Father

A child's willing acceptance of discipline reflects a core value of honor for that parent. No earthly parent feels honored when their child turns a "deaf ear" to their voice. It is no different with the Heavenly Father. In the Old Testament, Israel often refused to respond to God's correction and it grieved Him (Jer. 2:30). Listen to His words in Malachi 1:6-8: **"A son honors his father, and a servant his master. Then if I am a father, where is My honor? And if I am a master, where is My respect?"**

Israel's dishonor toward God as a Father manifested as *refusing His correction*. It also manifested itself by the *pitiful offerings* they brought instead of giving God their best and what He required. It is *right* that God should have requirements of His children and it *honors* Him when we give Him our best. It honors Him when we embrace His correction. Independence hates the yoke of discipline. But Father's discipline is the voice of truth and love that frees us from our ways (2 John 1:3). Proverbs 3:11 says: *Don't reject it! Don't hate it!*

Father God says that we have had earthly father's discipline us and we respected them—how much more should we revere His discipline that causes us to live. God *esteems* us as His beloved child by His discipline. He commands us to not lightly esteem His chastening or grow faint (Heb. 12:5-7, 9). He has great purposes for us—beyond our wildest imagination!

Disciplined for Holiness

Father God disciplines *all* who belong to Him. Some accept it, and some don't. But He says if we are *without* discipline, then we are illegitimate children and not true sons (Heb. 12:8-10). He also says that without discipline, we cannot share in His holiness, and without holiness we cannot know His glory. Discipline purifies our heart so that we can *see* Him and know His glory. His hand of correction puts in order those things in us that are out of order as the Father's Holy Spirit causes our spirit man to *be in sync* with His holiness. **The *Spirit of Holiness* is the *power* that raises us into divine purpose.**

We have a divine destiny that can only be realized through the disciplines of God. His discipline is not just about *us*, but is about His love for the world *through* us. The earth that has suffered beneath the sinful government of fallen man cries out for divine government through the sons and daughters of God. People are waiting to be healed and delivered from the curse under which they have labored. Who will be the polished arrow to be sent? Who is willing to go through the press to bring the Father's healing to those around them? We can have money, positions, and all that this world can give, but what does it mean if those around us are hurting and separate from God? What life can we truly have if we don't have Father's heartbeat in us?

Father, discipline me in Your love. Measure me with Your golden rod and make me a pure vessel for You through which You can bring healing to the earth.

Personal Application:

1. What was discipline like in your home growing up?
2. How do you respond to correction?
3. How do you respond to Father's discipline in your life?
4. Do you see your future? How do you need discipline for it?
5. List ways that Father teaches you to tread on serpents.

CHAPTER 9

Our Father's Work

Jesus said that whoever *fathers* us will determine the *works* we do—whether it be God, the flesh, or the devil (John 8:41; Gal. 5:19). At age twelve, the scene of young Jesus at the temple conversing with the priests showed that He knew, even then, God was His Father. **Knowing His identity, He embraced the Father's training and Spirit's leading that would shape His life and define His work.** In time, His work would revolutionize the seen and unseen world, forever.

Jesus said, *"My Father is working until now, and I Myself am working"* (John 5:17). He also said that the Father who was *in* Him, was the One who was doing the works *through* Him. If Father is working, and Jesus worked, then we must work. Father has a work to do not only *in* us, but *through* us. So pick up your gifts and call that God has given you—and let's work!

Our Work Begins in Prayer

"Our Father who is in heaven, hallowed be Your name,
Your kingdom come, Your will be done on earth as it is in heaven.

> Give us this day our daily bread and forgive us our debts
> as we forgive our debtors.
> And do not lead us into temptation, but deliver us from evil.
> For Yours is the kingdom and the power and the glory, forever.
> Amen."
> Matthew 6:9-13

We *cannot* do the work of God without a life rooted in prayer. The disciples of Jesus saw the importance He Himself put on prayer, and that the power of His life, work, and teaching was a result of the time He spent with Father. They also saw the anointing on John the Baptist's ministry and how he had taught his own disciples to pray. Jesus' disciples understood they were called to do a work with Him that could not be done in their own strength or ingenuity. They needed intimacy with the Father like Jesus had. So they asked Jesus to teach them to pray (Luke 11:1). So He did.

First, Jesus taught that prayer is fellowship with the Father—seeking His heart, Kingdom, and will, *first*, even before petitioning Him for personal needs. Prayer begins with the heart turning its attention to Father to *worship Him*. Prayer shuts the door to the voice of the flesh and circumstances as the spirit man gathers the whole heart and soul to come and revere Father as greater than all. Prayer presses in to know His heart and to discern *His* activity. Prayer is waiting on Him, as a child before an honored Father, to receive His instruction and counsel so that we say what He says and do what He shows us. Prayer is yielding our time, thoughts, voice, tears, and strength to Him. It is seeking *His* understanding and the fullness of His Spirit and power that His kingdom be manifest. Prayer is intercession for Father's will to be done on earth as it is in heaven. Prayer is about loving God.

Second, prayer includes bringing our personal needs to Him. He knows our needs, but He wants us to come into the fellowship of His love and *engage* with Him regarding the answer that will come in His time and way. Prayer is the *movement of faith* that looks to Father for all provision. It is *receiving* what has been given us in Christ—a place of sitting in Father's presence to listen and wait on Him (Eph. 2:4-6). As we listen, we hear; as we hear His voice, we then declare our agreement with Him—declaring His Word of authority into the situation of which we are praying. This sets spiritual dynamics in motion for earth to move with heaven.

Prayer is also repentance and asking to be washed from all sin and any area of unforgiveness. Prayer is seeking Father for protection and deliverance from all evil. Prayer is wrapped from beginning to end in adoration of the Father. It is not trying to compel an "unwilling God" to move, but is absolute confidence in Him as our caring Father, trusting that He who sees and hears, *will* answer.

The very act of putting things aside to take time with God is a declaration to our own flesh that its strength and ability is insufficient for the life and labor we are called to engage. Taking time for prayer cultivates an inward attitude that God alone is our source of life.

Prayer, however, isn't restricted to times alone with the Father. Prayer is a lifestyle. We are the temple of God and our communion with Him is 24/7 wherever we are. I am always aware of God. I pray when I get up, in the car, while I cook meals, as I study and work, and everywhere I go. We are called to a life of prayer that is continual fellowship with God and listening to His voice, wherever we are and whoever we are with.

Four basic points about prayer are:

- Prayer reveals the Fatherhood of God to us
- Prayer shows us the work He has for us to do
- Prayer prepares us for the work we are to do
- Prayer releases power for the work we are to do

The Work of Faith

While the foundation of our life and work is prayer, the work itself is that of *believing*. It is from the place of *believing* that flows the *acts* we do. Jesus said, "This is the work of God that you believe in Him whom He has sent" (John 6:29). "Truly, truly, I say to you, he who believes in Me, the works that I do, he will do also, and greater works than these he will do, because I go to the Father" (John 14:12).

Prayer positions the heart to hear from God. When God speaks, the *Spirit of faith* (the Holy Spirit) rests on His Word. When we hear His Word and engage with the Holy Spirit by coming into agreement with the Father and **acting on what He says**, power is released (Rom. 10:17). **This is what He calls "believing"**. Our *movement* with the Holy Spirit in accordance with God's speaking is called the *work of faith*.

Every work of God is empowered by the Holy Spirit because God's work is the expression of His Word upon which His Spirit rests. The Holy Spirit always moves on what Father says, and thus His movement in us *moves us* to also act on what Father says. Hearing God's voice may be a thought, an impression, a picture in our spirit, a feeling, a knowing or sensing we have, a Scripture we think of, or a word or words we hear inside us. And we are not the only ones who move on the Word of God—His angels do too: *"Bless the Lord, you His angels, mighty in strength, who perform His word, obeying the voice of His word!"* (Ps. 103:20)

In Luke 8, Jesus taught His followers that God's Word is like seed that He plants in our heart. **His purpose is that His Word becomes fruitful in us, producing a harvest that will glorify Him**. But look at what else happens when seed is planted: the enemy comes and tries to steal it before it takes root—Satan does not want God's Word to become fruitful in us. If the Word produces immediate joy, Satan will use difficulties and discouragement to sidetrack us and keep the Word from developing a strong root system, thus aborting a harvest; or if the Word grows into a plant, Satan will employ cares and pleasures to choke out life so that fruitfulness from the Word never comes to full fruition.

The god of this world has been defeated by God's Son, but he still works to try and abort the fruitfulness of God's Word and kingdom in our lives; he will do so wherever he is allowed to work unhindered. He seeks to destroy the rooting and maturing of God's Word in us because He knows the great harvest it will bring. The believing heart that hears the Word and *guards* the Word (with patience) will see it come to *full* fruition.

The fruitfulness of God's Word in us glorifies Him and is the mark of our devotion to Jesus (John 15:8). Our work is to co-labor with Jesus to govern the earth and destroy the works of darkness that steal the harvest of souls that belongs to God. Father redeemed man and the earth itself with the blood of His Son; the earth belongs to Him and the fullness of it, which includes a harvest of sons and daughters.

Continual listening to Father and doing His Word flames the fire of faith. Apathy and complacency are *in*actions that deny God's Word and cover us with a blanket of slumbering powerlessness. **Denying God's Word works death in us.** James 2 says that if faith does not engage with works, it is dead.

The movement of faith is initiated through love that moves us beyond ourselves and our own comforts (Gal. 5:6). When love is operating there is no complacency for love is a burning fire. Where there is love there is also *no fear,* for love drives out fear (1 John 4:18).

Our Appointed Work

As Father God sent His Son into the world as a minister of His kingdom, so the Son sends us (John 17:18; 20:21). We are appointed ministers of heaven to the earth (Luke 22:29). The word *"appointed"* means: to dispose one's affairs into the hands of another. What are these "affairs" we've been handed? *Preach the kingdom, heal the sick, raise the dead, cleanse the lepers, and cast out demons.* We are to *make disciples of all the nations*, baptizing them in the name of the Father, Son, and Holy Spirit, teaching them to know and do all that the Son has given us charge to do (Matt. 10:7-8; 28:18-20). Jesus said these things, including speaking with new tongues and having authority over deadly things, are signs that follow those who believe in His name (Mark 16:17, 18). However, this does *not* mean we go around picking up snakes or willfully drinking poison in order to "test" God!

We are commissioned as sons and daughters of God to do the same work that Jesus did. We are given the same Holy Spirit of *power* that He had to do the Father's work (Rom. 1:4; Acts 1:8; Rom.

15:19; 1 Cor. 5:4; 2 Tim. 1:7). After the sending of the Holy Spirit at Pentecost, the ministry of the Son is now through *His body—us*. **Our work with Christ in Kingdom affairs is both in *preaching and power* to heal, deliver, and restore people with the love of God.** Paul said that he did not minister simply in persuasive words of wisdom, but in *demonstration of the Spirit and of power* (1 Cor. 2:4). Some Christians believe that God doesn't heal today. I don't read anywhere that His Holy Spirit has left the earth! To not allow the Holy Spirit to move in power is to quench Him and limit Him. No one likes limitations. Do you?

The battle we face is with spiritual powers that hinder people from receiving the intimate knowledge of God. We cannot push back the powers of hell with merely good words and great programs. We need the *power* of the Holy Spirit to break the hold of Satan and minister restoration to people who are being held captive in darkness. We need the power of the Spirit to minister to the sick. We need the power of the Spirit to raise the dead. We need the power of the Spirit to minister divine truth and love that transforms a culture from darkness to light.

Divine Connection

As sons and daughters of God, we have divine authority to deliver those oppressed and possessed by demonic presence: spirits of sickness, error, witchcraft, bondage, fear, deafness, muteness, idolatry, seduction, lying, and perversion. Our commission as divine care-takers of the earth has never changed from the beginning; after the fall and prior to the cross we simply didn't have the power and authority for our commission—we had given it to the devil by our waywardness. But Jesus won it back and gave it to us as we have returned to Him. Now we have power and authority for our commission.

We were once in captivity, but now we are not. It's time to get up and act like it! We have the authority to command demons to go. Demons and fallen spirits are a part of this world; it's just a fact, and one we *must* deal with. We may not see them with the natural eye, but they are present and wreak terrible havoc, destroying lives, families, and nations where allowed to remain. Jesus discerned both the activity of the Holy Spirit and the work of the enemy. We are to do the same.

Some people are afraid to connect with God; some are afraid to connect with people. Some have a hard time connecting with themselves! Many things keep us in a place of *dis*connection, but remember, God is a God of community and connection. As ministers of His kingdom we are to connect heaven and earth. This is our call as kings and priests. **Disconnection must be replaced by connection with God and others.**

Everything the Son of Man did was motivated by love and was expressed through connecting with others. He didn't judge people, but He did judge and discern spirits that were operating in people. He dealt with spirits to free people, including His own disciple, Peter (Matt. 16:23). When we love and connect with people and discern the Spirit's activity, we become Father's vessels of mercy that minister life where there is death, light where there is darkness, and order where there is chaos.

Jesus said when we speak, it will not be our own words, but the *Spirit of the Father* speaking through us (Matt. 10:20). Father raises us up to be His healing voice to our generation. Father deeply cares for the life and destiny of *every* individual. He is interested in earth's welfare and everything that concerns what He created. He cares about crime, health, education, and businesses. He cares about people and nations that will one day stand before Him as they move into an eternal destiny. Will we work with Him for their well-being?

Our Specific Work

There are actions we engage because the Holy Spirit inspired *Word of God* instructs us to do them. They are the *general will of God* for everyone. There are also *appointed works*, such as we just mentioned, for every child of God. But there are also *specific works* we engage because the Father directs us individually regarding a specific location, work, or people group (remember, God's leading will always carry His heart, nature, and ways as revealed in His *written Word*). **Jesus did both the will and work of the Father.** He said they were His *food* (John 4:34).

I heard a pastor once say that to be truly effective in life, we must *specialize* in the work God gives us to do. Ephesians 4:16 says that every believer is a unique part of Christ's body—a member that supplies what is needed not only to mature the body, but to *hold* the body together. A physical body has individual parts that do *specific* works: a thumb doesn't do what an elbow does. And what my thumb does, it does really well! It's effective. It's not confused about its place or work. Many people I talk with and minister to don't seem to have a clear vision of what God wants them to do. They ask, "What is God's *will* for me?" But what they really want to know is God's *specific work* or purpose for them. His will is clearly written in His Word. So is the commission to heal, deliver, and raise the dead. But the specific work that involves gifts, talents, and specific calls is not clearly written, but is known by the voice of the Father as He speaks with us and orders our steps. Specific gifts and talents are simply tools that open doors for us to do our appointed work of the kingdom.

Jesus obeyed the Father and did His will and work in the place where God put Him. Deep down everyone wants purpose. We were created for it. The body of Christ longs to know the Father and do His work because the Spirit of adoption cries within them: *Here I am. What do You want me to do, Dad?*

To begin with, we have to believe that God still speaks. Some Christians believe that God stopped speaking when the last apostle died. I'm sorry they think their Father is mute. He is not. God's fathering in our life is very much connected to our hearing His voice. He will tell us what He wants us to do. He will direct our steps and give us the desires of our heart as we *delight in Him* (Ps. 37:4). He may speak to us in a dream about the work He has for us, or we may have a burden to minister to a specific people group. We may get a specific word in prayer or He may confirm through others a personal passion we have as His direction for us. Talents, abilities, and ideas for invention are also given by God for the work of His kingdom that He wants us to engage. **Those who minister through business are just as important as those who minister in the pulpit.**

Father's work for us may spring from a passion or desire He has put in us, or something we've gone through in the past as we become ministers of comfort with the same comfort He has given us. Our specific call, capacity, and geographical location may differ, but the same Holy Spirit empowers us for the Father's work.

The world is our mission field—we are all called to serve by doing God's will and work. Whatever Father speaks to us, He will also confirm it. He will bring divine connections and we will feel His anointing on what we do. In the 1981 British film, *Chariots of Fire*, a story based on Eric Liddell (a runner from Scotland who won the gold in the 1924 Summer Olympics), Eric Liddell said, "I believe that God made me for a purpose, but He also made me fast, and when I run, I feel His pleasure." Whether Eric Liddell really said that or not is not important, but the truth of it remains; **when we do the will and work of God we *feel* His pleasure.**

There is a deep satisfaction in the presence of God that accompanies co-laboring with Him. There is a pleasure in the anointing of the Holy Spirit that fills us as we engage our specific work from our Father. God told Moses, "My presence shall go with you, and I will give you rest" (Exod. 33:14). When Father gives us a specific work to do, His presence goes with us. We are not merely laboring, we are *co* laboring with Him. That is why it's important to get Father's direction and counsel for the work we do. And what we do with Him will be from a place of rest, not striving.

Father wants us to shine with His light and carry His anointing into *all* the world—into the education, media, business, government, and medical fields. He wants us to speak His good news, declare His peace, and demonstrate His love. God is stripping off religious mindsets that have taught us that ministry is limited to the pulpit. God's work through us is only limited by us, and not by the place He gives us to labor! He says, *"It's time for My people to rise up and carry My anointing that breaks every yoke into all the earth. It is time to shine with My glory in the work place and in the schools. Corporations need My glory! The arts need My glory! The shopping place needs My glory! The poor need My glory—go feed them!"*

I have been involved in music and teaching for many years, but currently the Father's *specific* work for me is writing. I've had a desire to write since I was twelve, but I am just now engaging this call. When I started this book, God gave me a dream. In the dream, my two children and I were sitting at school desks in a beautiful open meadow. There were rows of desks such as you would normally see in a classroom, but we were the only students. My children (now grown) appeared to be about seven and eight years old. The three of us were there to take a writing exam. A teacher sat before us at her desk and began timing. My children sailed through the exam while I, the writer in our family, struggled. At first, I wrote a full page with ease. But then I decided it wasn't quite right. I quickly erased it all and started over. This time, the words were strained. I wrote, erased, rewrote, erased again, and when the time was up, my paper showed only a few scribbled words. My kids were long gone and off playing happily. I went to the teacher who graciously said I could have more time. The dream ended.

When I woke up, I thought, *No! Nothing is going to hinder me any more!* What I felt the Father speak to me through that dream was that the hour is late, but I still have time to fulfill this specific work He's called me to do. He also wants me to not be hindered by perfectionism. While I am to seek excellence, His grace is to be my sufficiency. In my dream, my children represented childlikeness that obeys without a *fear of performance*. Stepping into the Father's work for us can be hindered if we focus on our own inadequacies or compare ourselves to others. No ability is too small when we put it in His hand. Father wants us free of such encumbrances so that we simply move in His love and leave the results to Him.

Look at Jesus, He was able to take five loaves of bread and two fishes and feed thousands of people, and have leftovers! **God uses our abilities, but He is not limited *to* our abilities or *by* our inabilities.** He can bring divine increase through whatever we give Him. We are also not to be hindered by the past. Today is a new day. I believe some of you reading this book have been waiting to step out into the things God has put in your heart to do. He says, *"It's time to get up, get dressed, and put on your strength. It's time to shake off the dust, put on beautiful clothing, and remove the chains of captivity from your neck. It's time to work!*" (Isa. 52:1-3, my version).

Father uses the humble to bring about His wonderful purposes and the "despised" to demonstrate His greatness (1 Cor. 1:28). Our work may be one-on-one or with larger groups, but the one thing that is important is that we follow Him. As we depend on *His* power and presence, His work through us *will* bear fruit that lasts forever (John 15:16).

The Reward for Our Labor

God promises that our diligent obedience *will* be rewarded. Father doesn't favor one person over another because of personality or ability; He loves and rewards each of us for our engagement with Him and faithfulness to do the work He gives us (1 Pet. 1:17). He is the *Rewarder* of those who diligently seek Him (Heb. 11:6). He even says that He is **not unjust** so as to *not reward* us for our labor (Heb. 6:10). He also promises that the *expectation* of our labor will not be cut off (Prov. 24:14).

Promises regarding labor and reward include:

- Reward comes to secret prayer and fasting (Matt. 6:6, 18)
- Ministering to prophets and righteous men and women makes you a partaker of their reward (Matt. 10:41)
- Ministering to the needy reaps reward (Matt. 10:42)
- Loving your enemies, doing good, and lending without return (Luke 6:35)
- Living for Christ will be rewarded with an inheritance (Col. 3:24)
- There is a *good* reward when a husband and wife labor together (Ecc. 4:9)

Our Abba Father knows that every work and field has many and varied challenges. He says, *"Do not be discouraged. Do not fear. Do not grow weary. You will reap in the appointed time"* (Gal. 6:9). Satan, who hates our labor and the resulting harvest that glorifies the Father, will try to discourage our expectation or make us feel our labor is in vain. But God justly rewards our obedience, so do not throw away your confidence! Continue sowing, watering, and cultivating those places where Father gives you to labor; whether with a child, your work environment, ministry, or wherever. Sow with a vision for the harvest. Sow specifically. Sow in prayer. Sow practically. Sow generously. Sow in faith, and seek God until He comes with heavenly rain that brings the increase to the seed you've sown (Hos. 10:12).

Sometimes we give up hope when we do not see the results we want. But sometimes the breakthrough is right around the corner! We must see with His perspective and not with our natural eyes. In Isaiah 41:10, God says, *"Do not fear, for I am with you; do not anxiously look about you, for I am your God. I will strengthen you, surely I will help you, surely I will uphold you with My righteous right hand."*

Be confident that He who gives the vision to sow, will also bring the rain for increase. Let your expectation be in Him alone (Ps. 62:5). If it seems the seed you've planted has failed to produce the desired harvest, remember, with God all things are possible to *him who believes* (Mark 9:23). Trust His time and His way; He is the faithful *Rewarder* and with Him there is *great* reward according to our labor (I Cor. 3:8; Heb. 10:35).

If we sow generously, we *will* reap generously (2 Cor. 9:6). We are not to envy the honor that others may be receiving and that we perhaps are not, nor compare the challenges in our own field to another's work. As Jesus said to Peter, ". . . what is it to you? You, follow Me!" (John 21:22 — Complete Jewish Bible).

Work and Motives

There are many works that we can engage: what **Father tells** us to do, what **others ask** us to do, and what **we want** to do. I must confess that I have wasted precious time, in the past, doing things that Father never called me to do. In so doing, I left the work He *did* call me to do undone. We can be busy doing things, even "ministry," that has nothing to do with Father's specific work for us. Such labor will not produce Father's intended harvest through our life. It won't even produce the "harvest" that *we* may personally be seeking. Work motivated by selfish ambition or the approval of man is empty and worthless.

I went through such a time. It was the smoke of "burnout" and the empty feeling I had inside that made me stop and listen to three questions resounding in me: ***What* am I doing? *Why* am I doing it? *Who* am I doing it for?** We can work really hard for the "kingdom," but what kingdom? What is our motive? Are we purpose-driven or led by the Spirit? Is our reward the pat-on-the-back? Our name mentioned well and often? Or do we move in loving obedience to His directives? We can do many things assuming we are pleasing God and yet completely miss it. Look at Paul, for example; before his divine encounter, he thought he was doing the will of God by killing the sons and daughters of God! Talk about missing it!

For me, it was a picture I saw in my spirit one afternoon that changed my perception and decisions regarding areas of ministry and service. I had a vision of all my labor, time, and effort being burned to ashes—labor that was not what Father had asked me to do. And in that moment I also saw hidden motives that were not pure. Scripture makes it clear that those who labor for personal gain will indeed get a reward, but not the desirable kind (Jude 11). Personally, I want a glorious reward.

Father says not to work to be seen of men (Matt. 6:2-5). If we do, we *may* reap their temporal applause, but when the day comes to stand before the Father what shall we present Him? A fruitful harvest resulting from obedience, or a smoldering field where the wood, hay, and stubble of self-effort lay burning?

We have kingdom affairs to attend. May we watch and work and not be sidetracked or discouraged lest the harvest fail. Jesus promised that if we overcome and keep His works to the end, we will sit with Him in His throne, just as He sits with Father in His throne (Rev. 3:21). What an incredible reward and future we have if we do the will and work of our Father!

Personal Application:

1. Whose works are manifest in your life?
2. What is the specific work Father wants you to do?
3. Do you need to learn to connect better with God or others? If so, ask the Holy Spirit to show you how; write down some goals.
4. What keeps you from stepping out into the work God has for you?
5. What are you doing? Why are you doing it? Who are you doing it for?

CHAPTER
10

The Father's Blessing

In Scripture, one of the most influential acts of a father toward his child was the spoken blessing. God Himself established the blessing as a way of ensuring the welfare and success of the next generation. God verbally blessed Adam and Eve as He appointed them rulers over the earth (Gen. 1:28). He blessed Noah and his sons after the flood. He blessed Abraham when He called him out of the world and into a new season of divine purpose (Gen. 12:1-3). And He blessed Jacob upon his return to the Promised Land. Jacob was so aware of the power of divine blessing that He literally wrestled with God for His impartation (Gen. 32:24-32). In the New Testament, we also see Abba Father blessing His Son at water baptism. The blessing was part of Father's equipping for the destiny Jesus was about to step into (Matt. 3:17).

In the Old Testament, God commanded Israel's priests and kings (both "fathering" positions), to bless His people because the blessing brought prosperity to live in the fulfillment of divine purpose. God wanted His people to be a *prosperous* nation that would bring *blessing* to the nations. God told Abraham, *"And I will make you a great nation, and I will bless you, and make your name great; and so you shall be a blessing"* (Gen. 12:2). The blessing of God is never meant to be self-gratifying, but to make His children to *be* a blessing to others.

God's High Priests were commanded to bless the sons of Israel saying:

"The Lord bless you, and keep you; the Lord make His face shine on you, and be gracious to you; The Lord lift up His countenance on you, and give you peace…
So they shall invoke My name on the sons of Israel, and I then will bless them." (Num. 6:22-27)

Did you catch that last statement? God said when the priest verbally released the word of blessing, it would summon the name of God over the children of Israel, and *then* God Himself would release the power of divine blessing from heaven. In this Scripture, we see God's blessing being *initiated* through the spoken word of His priests. We are priests unto God, and we are the body of Jesus the High Priest. We are Father's instruments of blessing! **The voice of *blessing* from spiritual leadership and fathers (who are priests of their home), is important for the prosperity of children.** The spoken blessing is important for the prosperity of God's children.

When Jesus, whose name is Everlasting Father, called His disciples *"the salt of the earth"* and *"the light of the world,"* **He was calling forth their destiny through blessing that contained power for increase.** The spoken blessing calls that which is not, as though it were. It calls into the seen realm, what is not yet seen. He began His training with His disciples by a series of *how* to walk in God's blessings (Matt. 5). The spoken blessing was also the last thing Jesus did before returning to heaven. That blessing released power for fruitfulness and increase for the apostolic commission to heal and disciple the nations (Luke 24:51). He blessed them to make them a blessing.

The Blessings of a Father

Words carry power. In the Old Testament, Jewish fathers and leaders understood the power of the spoken blessing and practiced it regularly by invoking *divine favor* upon a child, individual, or group. Their words were a coveted impartation for a life of increase. God Himself taught them the power of the blessing was to impact every area of life (see Deut. 28:1-14).

God's blessing of Abraham included a blessing on his lineage. Even Ishmael was blessed by God for fruitfulness, increase, and government. However, God's Covenant blessing and Messianic promise was reserved for Abraham's lineage through Isaac (Gen. 17:20-21). Isaac, in turn, blessed his sons, Jacob and Esau. While we have already seen Jacob's passion for the blessing in his mid-life years, we also read about it when, as a younger man, he deceived his father into speaking the firstborn blessing over him instead of over Esau (Gen. 27). While God had told their mother (while the two sons were still in her womb) that the older would serve the younger, Jacob connived for the blessing. While desiring the blessing (to be a blessing) is right, seeking a blessing through selfish ambition and deceit is the open door to every evil thing (James 3:16). God is able to give us His blessing in *His* way, and fulfill *all* His Word. He doesn't need our covetousness to help Him!

Before Jacob died, he also blessed his sons, as well as his grandsons, Ephraim and Manasseh (Gen. 49). Moses, too, as a "father" to the nation of Israel, blessed each of the twelve tribes (Deut. 33). King David also invoked the blessing of peace on the nation for he sought the *good* of the nation (Ps. 122:7-9). All these who spoke blessings did so with **expectation** of its divine effect in people's lives. Fulfillment of the blessing spoken over a child was the **expected norm** as they walked in obedience to the LORD.

Traditional Jewish fathers still, to this day, speak blessings over their children weekly, and practice special impartation as children move into young adulthood. A typical blessing includes the prayer that God would make their children "as Ephraim and Manasseh" which speaks of redemption and fruitfulness.

We may not have been blessed by a natural father, but Father God *has* blessed us with the firstborn blessing of His Son; all that is His is ours. We, who are born of the Spirit, are positioned for true prosperity because we are *in* Christ; He is the Blessed One of God (Matt. 21:9).

Positioned for Blessing and Prosperity

"Blessed be the God and Father of our Lord Jesus Christ, who has blessed us with every spiritual blessing *in the heavenly places* in Christ, just as He chose us in Him before the foundation of the world, that we would be holy and blameless before Him. In love He predestined us to adoption as sons through Jesus Christ to Himself, according to the kind intention of His will."
Ephesians 1:3, 5 (Emphasis added)

Blessings are spiritual in nature because they originate in the spirit realm (in heaven) and are manifest in earth. If we want manifest blessings, we must look to the One who sits in heavenly places—the One with whom we sit! (Eph. 2:6)

Father makes His blessing manifest in *every* aspect of our life including health, mental soundness, provision, finances, relationships, and guidance. His blessing is manifest in the presence of His joy, peace, and kindness. **Divine blessing overcomes anything that is working death in our spirit, soul, or body to make us prosperous.**

Children are a Parent's Inheritance and Reward

God said that children are both an *inheritance* and *reward*—therefore they are to be blessed (Ps. 127:3). No wonder Jesus took children up into His arms and blessed them (Mark 10:16). He was empowering God's inheritance for fruitfulness and increase!

Just as an earthly parent's greatest joy is to see their children blessed and successful, so it is with our Father in heaven. Having *many* royal sons and daughters, whose lives are rich in fruitfulness and authority, makes a *full inheritance* and *rich reward* for Him.

In light of what Father teaches us, all parents should bless their children regularly with peace, wisdom, a prayer for divine guidance, and protection from evil. Leaders should bless those under their leadership. This is the Father's heart from generation to generation. People should be blessed into their destiny! As a child is prosperous, their prosperity becomes a *blessing* to the fathers and leaders who have trained them.

A father's blessing is the act of a father seeing the destiny of a child and calling it out. A father's blessing awakens the callings and gifts within his children.

I am not alone in saying that I have experienced the pain that results from a spiritual leader's cursing over God's children. But I have also experienced the healing impartation of a spiritual father's blessing. For the past ten years, my husband and I have enjoyed the privilege of being in a local church where not only does the leadership bless the people, but the people are taught to bless one another. Imagine that—Christians who bless one another! When the Lord led our family to be a part of *River of Glory* in Plano, Texas, we were in a time of healing from abuse that had taken place in a previous church. When we came to the "*River*," it was the first time I had seen the spoken blessing demonstrated—and I have been in church all my life! The pastor would often take time to lay hands on the people and impart blessing. Now, the people *bless one another* as a regular part of church services. And not only that, but they are taught to minister the blessing of God wherever they go.

The imparted blessing has not only brought healing to our lives, but gifts and callings in my life have been awakened. This is what the blessing does. Abuse shuts people down, including their gifts and their calling. But the blessing brings increase! I have seen *countless* lives restored and become fruitful through the power of love and spoken blessing.

The following are some general facts about the blessing:

- It is verbal—not merely a wish or desire (Gen. 1:28)
- It is given by Father God to His children (Gen. 1:28; Matt. 25:34; Ps. 3:8)

- It is released where there is unity of God's children (Ps. 133:3)
- It manifests through increase and authority (Mark 8:7; Matt. 24:46)
- It is evidenced in covenant with God (Isa. 61:9; Isa. 44:3)
- It is God's manifest favor upon His people (Ezek. 34:26)
- It releases joy (Ps. 21:6)
- It is found in the blood of Christ (1 Cor. 10:16)
- It exalts a city (Prov. 11:11)
- It makes one rich and He adds no sorrow to it (Prov. 10:22)
- It cannot be revoked once given (Gen. 27:33; Num. 23:20)
- It is released through obedience so that we are (Deut. 28:1-14):
    - Overtaken by the blessing of God
    - Blessed wherever we go
    - Blessed with children who are blessed
    - Blessed with provision
    - Abundantly prosperous
    - Blessed as the head and not the tail
    - Blessed with favor to enter places where others cannot go
    - Renowned as a people set apart for God
    - Blessed with victory when enemies rise against us
    - Blessed with an open storehouse in heaven
    - Blessed with rain that brings increase
    - Blessed in the work of our hand
    - Blessed as givers, not borrowers

The spoken blessing is given with divine purpose:

- To make us a blessing (Gen. 12:2; 22:17-18)
- To fulfill our commission with increase and authority (Gen. 1:27-28; 35:11-12; Matt. 14:19)
- For the manifestation of God's glory (Lev. 9:22-24)
- To call out prophetic destiny (Gen. 24:60; 27: 27-29; Deut. 33)
- To change our nature and make us fruitful (Gen. 35:9-12)

Making Our Life "Blessable"

The recipient of the blessing also has responsibility for the blessing to be *effectual*. As children, we have our part in making our life one upon which God's blessing can *rest* with effectiveness. We cannot continue in sin *and* expect divine prosperity. We saw how Jacob had an inherent hunger for the blessing, but divine blessing required humility. As Jacob wrestled with God to be blessed, God touched Jacob's thigh in a way that brought *manifest change to his walk* (Gen. 32). He was never the same. God's touch caused Jacob to walk more *humbly*. **Making our life "blessable" isn't about *trying* to be perfect, but about *engaging* with God and letting His presence change us.**

We want God's blessing, but are we willing for His presence to touch us and change how we walk? Are we willing to walk humbly with God? Humility transforms our life into one that is blessed. Jesus, the **Blessed One**, said, *"Learn of Me; for I am meek and lowly in heart"* (Matt. 11:29).

Actions that engage with God and release His blessing are:

- Faith in God's Word (Gal. 3:9; Luke 1:45)
- Believing *before* seeing (John 20:29)
- The fear of the Lord (Ps. 112:1; Ps. 128:1, 4)
- Delighting in, and meditating on, God's Word (Ps. 1:1-3)
- Trusting God and making Him our source (Ps. 2:12; 34:8; 84:5, 12)
- Being forgiven by God (Ps. 32:1; Rom. 4:7, 8)
- Practicing righteousness (Ps. 106:3; Ps. 112:2)
- Refusing offense (Luke 7:23)
- Steadfastness with God (Ps. 40:4)
- Moral purity and purity of heart (Ps. 24:3-5; Ps. 119:1)
- Sharing with the poor, being generous (Ps. 41:1; Prov. 11:25; 22:9)
- Ministering to the poor and handicapped (Luke 14:12-14)
- Honoring spiritual leaders with your *firstfruits* (Ezek. 44:30)

- Abiding in God's presence (Ps. 65:4; 84:4)
- Continual praise and thanksgiving (Ps. 84:4)
- Allowing God to discipline us and instruct us from His Word (Ps. 94:12)
- Seeking God with the whole heart (Ps. 119:2)
- Following the ways of wisdom (Prov. 8:32-33)
- Waiting on God's timing to bring things about (Prov. 20:21)
- Faithful stewardship (Luke 12:43; Prov. 28:20)
- Believing and declaring what God says (Matt. 16:17)
- Persevering under trial (James 1:12)
- Believing the prophecy of the book of Revelation (Rev. 1:3)
- Hearing and obeying God (Deut. 29:9; Exod. 39:43; 1 Chron. 22:13; Luke 11:28)
- Having our garments washed (Rev. 22:14)
- Seeking the peace of Jerusalem (Ps. 122:6)

Things That Hinder the Blessing

The opposite of the blessing is the *curse*. A curse causes withering and "fruitlessness". Attitudes and actions that we engage can make place in our life for the curse to operate instead of God's blessing. (Prov. 26:2).

Things that not only hinder the blessing, but invoke the curse include:

1. Disobedience to God's Word (Deut. 28:15-45)
2. Adultery (Prov. 22:14)
3. Falling away from God (Heb. 6:4-8)
4. Living by the works of the law as *means* of salvation (Gal. 3:10, 13)
5. Not listening to God and not honoring Him (Mal. 2:2)
6. Robbing God of tithes and offerings (Mal. 3:8-9)
7. Putting trust in man and the flesh (Jer. 17:5)
8. Negligence in doing Father's will (Jer. 48:10)
9. Cowardice in battle (Jer. 48:10)

The Blessing that Belongs to the Father

Father God says that He *delights* over us to prosper and bless us (Deut. 28:63). He even says that He *teaches* us to prosper! (Gen. 39:3) But it's important to know all of what Father says about prosperity and blessing. **Scripture instructs us that the first *portion* of increase and fruitfulness *belongs* to God, that being the tithe** (Lev. 27:30). This includes income as well as produce, livestock, and offspring. Psalm 115:18 says, *"But as for us, we will bless the Lord from this time forth and forever..."* We bless God, not just with our words, or even talents, but with our finances, too. We bless Him with obedience regarding the *tithe* (the first ten percent of our income that He says *belongs* to Him). We also bless Him with *offerings* (what we give *after* the tithe). Blessing Father with our finances is *right conduct* as His children. He is *worthy* to be blessed by what He gives us. Withholding tithe and offerings is a dishonor to Him. If we withhold from Him, He will withhold from us.

Sharing the Blessing

During the U.S. presidential election of 2008, a comment was made about "sharing the wealth." While the U.S. government was not founded on principles that "mandate" sharing such as socialism does, caring for the poor and the sick *is* a command given to the Church by God. Such a command requires finances provided through hands that are willing to give. At the time of this writing, America (and many other countries) is in a financial crisis because of covetousness at every level of government and corporate business. America also has a health care crisis promoted by greed. Many of God's people are also caught in a web of greed which is defined as: an overwhelming desire to have more of something, such as money, than is actually needed.

Our *heavenly mandate* to care for the poor and needy can only happen as our hearts are free from greed so that the financial blessing that Father gives us can be used to bless others. God doesn't need our money, but He does want our heart, and purchasing needed supplies for the poor and support of His ministry does require finances. Even Jesus had finances given to support His ministry! (Luke 8:3)

Jesus instructed His disciples both to *take money* and *not take money* with them as they travelled and ministered (Luke 22:35-36). He taught both because while they needed to learn that their sufficiency was of God—not what was in their coin purse—finances *were* needed to bless others. We must learn this, too. The disciples had already witnessed the demise of one comrade whose heart was controlled by covetousness (John 12:6). Watch what God allows to be put in your hand—money is power and can be a blessing or a downfall. 1 Timothy 6:10 says that the *love of money* is the root of all evil. Money isn't evil, but covetousness is.

In the New Testament, we see different ways of how people relate to money. The church congregation at that time would bring money to the apostles for them to distribute to the poor. However, people who *lied* about money were struck dead by God! (Acts 4:35; 5) While God desires a cheerful giver, lying about finances brings heaven's wrath.

One of the *kingdom parables* told by Jesus was about the lord who entrusted money to his servant for the purpose of sowing it and increasing it for his (the master's) household. One servant, instead of seeking wisdom in how to multiply it, buried it. He was punished as an unfaithful servant (Matt. 25). God's Word has a lot to say about finances. Our financial dealings are an important issue with our Father.

The days we are living in requires a shift in how we relate to money as God's children. Father wants to teach us a new paradigm of how to relate to finances *through* His wisdom and counsel, *for* the benefit of kingdom work, *with* a heart that is free from greed. As Christians, our thinking regarding money must be rooted in heavenly places, not earthly mindsets.

I love America. I love our beautiful and spacious homes that reflect abundance and enlargement—qualities that express heaven. But much of what we have is an *appearance* of wealth that is built on debt. God wants us to live in *true* prosperity, not covetousness and debt. The blessing that has been given us has too often blessed our own comfort rather than ministering to the poor, fatherless, and widow. It is time for earthly wisdom to be replaced with the mind of Christ. Like Jacob, our walk needs to be changed for a new day of kingdom blessing.

Statistics say that a meager 5% of adult Americans tithe. **Doug Hagedorn of *Financial Foundations Builders* reports that we are more prosperous as a nation and individuals than ever before, yet, we give less, are more counseled, more divorced, and more in debt than any previous generation.** Charitable giving is a mere 2.6 % as people are paying more in yearly credit interest than in yearly giving.[1]

Our Father will not be mocked. If we do not honor Him with our finances, how can He bless us financially? God wants to open the store house of heaven, but He wants us to be a *conduit* of His supply, not a black hole!

Blessing Requirements and Fulfillment

Some blessings have *specific* requirements to be fulfilled for *specific* blessing to be released:

Requirement—Fulfillment

We obey the Lord—we are overtaken by blessing (Deut. 28:1-13)
We believe God—He performs His Word in us (Luke 1:45)
We are poor in Spirit—the kingdom of heaven is ours (Matt. 5:3, 5)
We mourn—We receive comfort (Matt. 5:4)
We are meek—We inherit the earth (Matt. 5:5)
We hunger and thirst for righteousness—We are satisfied (Matt. 5:6)
We show mercy—We obtain mercy (Matt. 5:7)
We are pure in heart—We will see God (Matt. 5:8)
We are a peacemaker—We are known as God's son (Matt. 5:9)
We are persecuted for righteousness—We inherit the kingdom (Matt. 5:10, 11)
We watch for His return—We sit and dine with Jesus (Luke 12:37)
We bless the poor and needy—We receive eternal reward (Luke 14:14)

We persevere under trial — We receive the crown of life (James 1:12)
Our robes are washed — We eat from the tree of life (Rev. 22:14)

The Blessing and God's Presence

Blessing and prosperity have always been a part of God's manifest presence with His covenant people. It is a testimony of His goodness and *who* He is to those who love and serve Him. In Scripture, God's presence is associated with provision. All through the Old Testament, as God's covenant people walked with Him they were prosperous *and* victorious against their enemies. Even in times of famine, God would designate places for His people to prosper. As they obeyed His voice, they increased (Gen. 26:1-12). As long as God's people worshipped Him and kept themselves from idols, His blessing rested on them. Only in times of judgment for continued waywardness was blessing removed.

What about poor nations where Christians live in poverty? Well, first, maybe there wouldn't be so much poverty if we "shared the wealth"! Second, Jesus said to go and *teach* the nations *all* that He has commanded. This includes the power of divine blessing. Will you go teach them? What about those who suffer for the sake of the gospel? Those who suffer for the sake of the gospel *will* be rewarded.

Some Christians seek prosperity for personal gain while others shun *any* thought of prosperity. Father wants us to be prosperous, but for His glory, not for selfish gain. Remember too, prosperity is not just about money, but manifests in myriad ways. God's Word promises that the one who trusts God *will* be blessed and prosper (Prov. 28:25). A life rooted in loving dependence on God prospers (Judg. 17:13). God's presence causes us to prosper as triumphant against enemy rule in our life (2 Kings 18:7). Seeking God and doing His will, *with all our heart*, causes us to prosper (2 Chron. 31:21). Listen to this promise: the one who fears the Lord will be taught of the Lord and his *soul* will *abide* in prosperity (Ps. 25:13). 3 John 1:2 says that even our *health* prospers as our *soul* prospers.

Father delights in the prosperity of those who serve Him (Ps. 35:27). As God's heritage, we are generous givers of whatever we have because the nature of our Father dwells in us. He is a giving God! Psalm 37:11 says that the *humble* prosper with Father's blessings and obtain promises. **God leads His children not only *out* of bondage, but *into* prosperity** (Ps. 68:6). He rewards the righteous with prosperity (Prov. 13:21). Our Father promises that the weapons formed against us by the enemy will *not* prosper; He has also given us authority to condemn every tongue that accuses us—this is our heritage! (Isa. 54:17)

Blessing One Another

Father is so zealous for His children to walk in blessing, that He literally blesses those who bless us and curses those who curse us (Gen. 12:3). That is a covenant promise. If necessary, He will even use angels with swords and talking donkeys to stop a person sent to curse us! (Num. 22:23) **Why such zealousness on God's part? Because divine blessing is not simply about *us*, but is given to us that we might fulfill Father's work in the earth.**

James 3:9-10 says we are to bless and *not* curse! Christians should never curse or verbally abuse any other human being. Father commands us to bless and not curse—including those who curse, mistreat, and persecute us (Luke 6:28; Rom. 12:14). He says not to return evil for evil, or insult for insult (1 Pet. 3:9). What? Speak fruitfulness and increase into their lives? Yes! How about blessing them with love and a prayer for increase in divine revelation, grace, and salvation? We all go through times when we may feel mistreated, misunderstood, or misjudged. It is part of life on earth! What are we to do? Pray the love of God on the person who has hurt us. When we are merciful toward others who mistreat us, we reap a harvest of blessing and mercy on our own life. *"Blessed are the merciful, for they shall receive mercy"* (Matt. 5:7).

Using our mouth in a way that pleases Father includes practicing right *"self-talk"*—you know—the words that unconsciously slip out of our mouth about us. Some people do not have a problem in this area. Some do. Saying things like: *I'm just stupid, I hate myself, I'm a misfit, I'll never make it, no one loves me, I'm a failure*, or any other negative declaration against ourselves is self-cursing and is from the pit of hell. As a young person, I spoke such words. But as Father has taught me how *He* sees me and that I am to use my mouth for *His* words, I now try to speak words that agree with Him, not with hell. Our mouth was given to us to be a tool in the hand of God, not the world, the flesh, or the devil!

Impartation of Blessing

You may have never received a spoken blessing from an earthly parent, but God, as your Parent, says *you are blessed* in His Son. Father sees your future, and He *will* bring about His good purposes in your life. Look at the life of David—he wasn't even recognized by his own father when the prophet came to anoint him to be king of Israel! (1 Sam. 16) But Father blesses you as His dear child for His purposes, and no one can stop it!

> **"'For I know the plans that I have for you',
> declares the LORD,
> 'plans for welfare and not for calamity
> to give you a future and a hope.'"
> Jeremiah 29:11**

You are Papa's treasured child. If you need to repent of self-cursing, then do so now.

Pray: *Father, You love me so much. You created me in Your own image. You reached down into the midst of my darkness and pulled me into Your wonderful light. I repent of any words I have spoken that have demeaned, despised, dishonored, or rejected who I am. I come into agreement with You and how You see me. I bind all spirits of self-hatred or unforgiveness toward myself and loose them from me now. I ask You, Holy Spirit, to go to the root of every lie I have believed and show me the truth. I break agreement now with every unrighteous way of thinking. Father, thank You that I am blessed of*

You. I decree that I am accepted in the Beloved, and I am loved by You, Dad. In You, I have no lack. In Jesus' name, Amen.

And now, I would like to speak a blessing over you: The Lord bless you, and make His face to shine on you, and be gracious to you. The Lord give you peace and fill you with His Spirit of glory. The Lord bless you with strength, hope, provision, life, confidence, and health. The Lord bless you by rooting you and grounding you in His love. The Lord bless you with fruitfulness and increase. May the Father of glory bless you with the Spirit of wisdom and revelation in the intimate knowledge of His Son, and with eyes that see the plans and purposes of God toward you. The Lord bless you in the knowledge of the surpassing greatness of His power in you and over you, and with the Spirit of understanding of His great inheritance in *you* and your life!

Personal Application:

1. In what ways do you see Father God's blessing in your life?
2. How are you blessing Father with your income?
3. *What is your self-talk like?*
4. In what ways can you release Father's blessing to others? List them.

CHAPTER 11

For Love of the Father

What we have learned brings us to the understanding that the Father's love is where it all begins and ends. A child's very existence is the fruit of love. We are the fruit of God's love. We come from Him, we belong to Him, and one day we will see Him *face to face*. Meanwhile, His Spirit in us journeys us into our divine destiny—His presence shaping our life for His rich purposes. The Father's love is the divine spring from which all of life is meant to flow. Through the abiding of the *Spirit of the Son* within us, our life can now be lived, not for self, but for the love of the Father. We love Him because He first loved us!

Jesus walked on earth with a heart that beat with love for His Father *and* love for us—Their creation. Love wasn't just the Son's core-value, it was the nature that motivated all He did and said as He drank from the fountain of Abba Father's love. All His actions and words ministered the *Living Water* and *Bread of Life* to mankind, while at the same time, the *fire* of divine love in Him worked to destroy everything that separated us from love. His death and resurrection has given us a new framework to live by as a life filled with love through fellowship with the Father, Son, and Holy Spirit.

In our Father's kingdom, everything is rooted in love and expressed through *serving*. The Son of Man came to *serve*, not to be served, and to *give His life* as a ransom for many (Matt. 20:28). **The cross and resurrection of Christ opened the way for us to return to a life of being fathered by God for a divine purpose, a life that engages with Abba Father regarding His plans for our homes, communities, and nations.** This is what the Son did.

As the children of God, our life is to be rooted in love that serves. The fall of man was a fall *away* from the love of God; salvation is a return to the love of God. *Love is not self-seeking.* Love seeks the honor of God and the well-being of mankind. At the celebration of the last supper, Jesus prayed, asking that just as Father had loved Him, we would know that *same love* (John 17:26). He also prayed that we would *love one another* with the *same love* that Jesus Himself loves us (John 15:9-12).

Life isn't about things or positions. It isn't about pleasures or powers. **Life isn't about what we *get*, but what we *give*.** And what Father has for us to give is laced with *eternity*, that being, the heartbeat of eternal life found in the intimate knowledge of God. Even temporal things we give to others, like food, shelter, and a helping hand, is laced with eternity when given by a loving hand anointed by the Spirit of God. As we serve and decree the blessing of God into our surroundings, lives are changed. Our new framework of community with the Father, Son, and the Holy Spirit infuses eternity into everything we do; business becomes a place for Father's presence to be known, and talents become a tool for the Holy Spirit to flow through; all of life becomes a venue through which the Son can minister the Father's kingdom through us to a darkened world.

When we are filled with Father's love, everything we do will spring from the fire of love. The Son loved the Father more than His own life which He laid down for us. This is the same glory and image into which we are being transformed: vision that burns with the fire of compassion, feet that burn with judgment against injustice, and a mouth that wields truth in love to sever every lie and release the healing waters of God (Rev. 1).

Love Made Perfect

As brothers and sisters in Christ, our love for each other is the evidence by which the world knows we believe in Jesus (John 13:35). 1 John 2:5 says that God's love is perfected in us by doing what He says in His Word. Loving God is *perfected* by revering the Father's Voice as the counsel we embrace, the wisdom we seek, and the knowledge we act on. The spirit of the world does not revere Father's Voice, but rather it opposes Him. But the sons and daughters of God are *"animated by the same Spirit"* by which Jesus is animated—a Spirit of being one with the Father.

The love of self made us *powerless*, but the love of God now *empowers* us for a divine destiny. Scripture says if we love the world and its ways, then the love of the Father is not in us. James 4:4 says that *friendship* with the spirit of the world makes us to be at enmity (hostile) toward God. All that is in the world, the lust of the flesh and the lust of the eyes, and the boastful pride of life, is not from the Father, but is from the world, and the world is passing away. However, the one who does God's will lives forever (1 John 2:15-17). Jesus came to destroy the *lawlessness* of sin that drives man away from the will of God. He came to write on our hearts the *law* of God, which is the law of love that obeys the will of God and does His work. Love is made perfect by abiding in the teachings of Christ; in so doing, we *have* the Father and the Son dwelling in us (2 John 1:9).

Love and the Mind of Christ

In the book of Revelation, we read of the vision of the end-times given to the apostle John as he was taken to heaven. There he saw the beast, the dragon, and the false prophet. He saw how the Antichrist would operate and war against God's people. He saw end-time destruction and devastation ravaging the earth because of that spirit. John saw it operating not only in the leaders of nations, but in the people of those nations. He identified it as the rejection of Jesus Christ as Lord, and thus a rejection of the Father. This is what it means, he said, to deny the Father and the Son (1 John 2:22, 23). This is the *spirit of antichrist* at work.

However, John also saw 144,000 with the *Father's name written in their foreheads*. We talk about the mark of the beast, but Father's children also have a mark on their forehead; it is God's name. The forehead symbolizes mindsets and belief systems that direct our choices and behavior. Jesus may not have had a physical mark on His forehead, but His mind was etched with a burning love for the Father and His words.

In the Old Testament, High Priests wore a turban bearing a platelet across the forehead that read *"Holiness to the Lord"* (Exod. 28:36-38). As we have previously noted, the word *"holiness"* means *"set apart."* Jesus is our High Priest and His *forehead* has inscribed on it *"set apart for God."* **No wonder God's Word says we are to have the mind of Christ—a mind that is governed by the Father's love and name.** Our mind does not belong to the world, the flesh, or the devil. Our mind is set apart for God so that we move with His Word at our helm. Salvation in Christ is our helmet that governs us into divine destiny, keeping our thoughts rooted in the Father's love.

For the Love of Our Father

There is a day coming when the world will fear, and chaos will abound on every side as the nations rise against God and His anointed. There will be a great apostasy—a falling away from the love of God by many. But there will also be a great host of the redeemed, who are even now rising up with a single eye focused on One—the Redeemer who has brought us into fellowship with the Father. These who have been redeemed from death are the ones who will do the greater works of Christ; they will be strong and do exploits because they know their God. They will move as a *heavenly troop* doing the Father's will on earth as it is in Heaven. These are the sons and daughters of God.

We have not been left fatherless in this world. If we live as "Fatherless" it is either by choice or ignorance. It isn't enough to know that God is *a* Father, but that He is *our* Father—Jesus' Father,

Being Fathered for a Divine Purpose

your Father, and mine. Life is meant to be lived through intimate fellowship with God as our *Dad*, our *Papa*, who is daily training and fathering us for a divine purpose. 1 Peter 1:17 says that if we claim God as our Father, then we must be careful to revere and honor Him as such *"during our stay on earth."* In doing so, we understand that we will receive our reward accordingly. Just as earthly fathers are rewarded for their labor by children who honor their training, so God is rewarded by the honor we give Him through a life that glorifies Him. May we never lose sight of the great privilege we have of being called *God's children* (1 John 3:1).

I pray that after reading these pages, you have encountered a deeper place of knowing the Father, Son, and Holy Spirit *who see your future* and are working intimately with you for a full destiny in divine purpose. May your life be rooted and grounded in Christ's love, and may you minister eternity wherever you go by the abiding of the Spirit, doing all things for the love of the Father.

The Father loves you.

Personal Application:

1. What is the "spring" that motivates your choices and decisions?
2. What does loving others look like to you?
3. Have you experienced times when acts of love made you sense the power of the Holy Spirit, or times when selfishness made you feel "powerless"?
4. What is most often at the helm of your thoughts?
5. Do you know how much Father God loves you?

Notes

Chapter 1

1. Fred H. Wright, *Manners and Customs of Bible Lands,* Chicago: Moody Press, 1953, pp. 103, 118.
2. Some concepts of family roles taken from *Sozo* ministry, Bethel Church, Redding, California

Chapter 2

1. Source: www.dads4kids.com/facts on fatherless kids, and www.fathersunite.org, July, 2008.

Chapter 3

1. Gary Chapman, *The Five Love Languages of Teenagers,* Chicago: Northfield Publishing, 2000.

Chapter 4

1. Walter A. Elwell, *Baker Theological Dictionary of the Bible,* "Fatherhood of God," Grand Rapids Michigan: Baker Books, 1996, p. 247.

Chapter 6

1. *Streams in the Dessert* Vol. 1. Grand Rapids, Michigan: Zondervan Publishing House, 1925, excerpt July 16th

2. *Streams in the Dessert* Vol. 1. Grand Rapids, Michigan: Zondervan Publishing House, 1925, excerpt Sept. 24th

Chapter 10

1. http://www.kluth.org/church/Financialtrends1950-2000.htm. November 4, 2008. Site references Doug Hagedorn's book, *Ease the Squeeze*.

Notes

Chapter 1

1. Fred H. Wright, *Manners and Customs of Bible Lands*, Chicago: Moody Press, 1953, pp. 103, 118.
2. Some concepts of family roles taken from *Sozo* ministry, Bethel Church, Redding, California

Chapter 2

1. Source: www.dads4kids.com/facts on fatherless kids, and www.fathersunite.org, July, 2008.

Chapter 3

1. Gary Chapman, *The Five Love Languages of Teenagers*, Chicago: Northfield Publishing, 2000.

Chapter 4

1. Walter A. Elwell, *Baker Theological Dictionary of the Bible*, "Fatherhood of God," Grand Rapids Michigan: Baker Books, 1996, p. 247.

Chapter 6

1. *Streams in the Dessert* Vol. 1. Grand Rapids, Michigan: Zondervan Publishing House, 1925, excerpt July 16th

2. *Streams in the Dessert* Vol. 1. Grand Rapids, Michigan: Zondervan Publishing House, 1925, excerpt Sept. 24th

Chapter 10

1. http://www.kluth.org/church/Financialtrends1950-2000.htm. November 4, 2008. Site references Doug Hagedorn's book, *Ease the Squeeze*.

KNOWING GOD'S NAME

There are many names in Scripture that describe God. A name speaks of one's nature. To know God's name is to know Him. The following are just a few of God's names.

I Am—the Self Existing One (Exod. 3:14)
Jehovah—the One who is (Gen. 2:7)
Jehovah-jireh—God who provides (Gen. 22:14; Phil. 4:19)
Jehovah-rapha—God who heals (Exod. 15:26)
Jehovah-nissi—God is my banner (Exod. 17:15; 2 Chron. 20:17)
Jehovah-m'kaddesh—God who sanctifies and sets me apart (Lev. 20:7)
Jehovah-shalom—God of peace (Judg. 6:24; Isa. 26:3)
Jehovah-tsidkenu—God our righteousness (Jer. 23:5-6; Gal. 3:6)
Jehovah-rohi—God my Shepherd (Ps. 23:1)
Jehovah-shammah—God who is there (Eze. 48:35; Ps. 139:7-8)
Elroi—God who sees me (Gen. 16:13)
Holy God (Josh. 24:19)
Almighty (Gen. 17:1)
Eternal God (Deut. 33:27)
Judge (Gen. 18:25)
Living God (Josh. 3:10)
Incorruptible God (Rom. 1:23)
Forgiving God (Neh. 9:17; Ps. 99:8)

God of all Comfort (2 Cor. 1:3)
God of all Grace (1 Pet. 5:10)
God of Peace (Isa. 9:6; Acts 5:30)
God of Truth (Ps. 31:5; Isa. 65:16)
God who avenges (Ps. 94:1)
Great & Powerful God (Neh. 1:5)
Deliverer (2 Sam. 22:17-20)
Loving God (John 3:16)
The Only Wise God (Rom. 16:27)
Defender (Ps. 68:5)
Miracle working God (Ps. 77:14)
God my Husband (Isa. 54:5)
God my Stronghold (Ps. 18:1-3)
Mighty Warrior (Jer. 20:11)
Ever-Present Help (Ps. 46:1; 33:20)
Father of Compassion (2 Cor. 1:3)
My Shield (2 Sam. 22:3)
Redeemer (Isa. 49:7)
Rescuer (Ps. 140:1)
Refiner (Ps. 66:10)

Other books by J. Nicole Williamson

Freedom in the Light — A Christian Twelve Step

To order a copy visit:
www.hydrohouseministry.com

Printed in the United States
135171LV00002B/4/P